W9-ACB-112

MAKING THEATER

MAKING THEATER
Developing Plays with Young People

•

Herbert R. Kohl

Teachers & Writers Collaborative
New York, N.Y.

Making Theater

Teachers & Writers Collaborative
5 Union Square West
New York, N.Y. 10003

Library of Congress Cataloging-in-Publication Data

Kohl, Herbert R.
  Making theater.

  1. Children's theater—Presentation, etc.
2. Theater—Study and teaching. I. Title
PN3157.K64 1988   792'.0226   88—16010
ISBN 0-915924-16-1
ISBN 0-915924-17-X (pbk.)

Printed by Philmark Lithographics, New York, N.Y.

Contents

Acknowledgments

Ursula K. Le Guin, excerpted from *Very Far Away from Anywhere Else*. Copyright © 1976 Ursula K. Le Guin. Reprinted with the permission of Atheneum Publishers, an imprint of MacMillan Publishing Company.

Excerpt from *The Ugly Duckling* by A.A. Milne reprinted by permission of Curtis Brown Ltd., London. Copyright © 1941 by A.A. Milne.

Excerpt from *Harvey*. Copyright © 1943 by Mary Chase (under the title *The White Rabbit*). Copyright renewed, 1970, by Mary C. Chase. Copyright © 1944 by Marcy C. Chase (under the title *Harvey*). Reprinted by permission of the Dramatists Play Service, Inc. and the estate of the author.

Opening monologue from Act I in *Amadeus* by Peter Shaffer copyright © 1980, 1981 by Peter Shaffer. Reprinted by permission of Harper & Row Publishers, Inc.

Excerpt from *The King Who Took Sunshine* by James Reeves reprinted by permission of William Heinemann, Ltd.

Selection from *The Growing Pains of Adrian Mole* by Sue Townsend reprinted by permission of Methuen & Co. Ltd., London.

Excerpt from *The Member of the Wedding* by Carson McCullers. Copyright © 1951 by Carson McCullers. Reprinted by permission of New Directions Publishing Corporation.

Excerpt from *Under Milk Wood* by Dylan Thomas. Copyright © 1954 by New Directions Publishing Corporation. Reprinted by permission of New Directions.

Excerpt from *A Woman Alone* by Dario Fo and Franca Rame used by permission of Pluto Press, Ltd.

Selection from *Shakespeare's Stories*. Copyright © 1985 Leon Garfield. Reprinted by permission of Schocken Books, published by Pantheon Books, a division of Random House, Inc.

"The Little Girl and the Wolf" by James Thurber. Copyright © 1960 by James Thurber. From *A Thurber Carnival*, acting edition, published by Samuel French, Inc.

When learning's triumph o'er her barb'rous foes
First reared the stage, immortal Shakespeare rose;
Each change of many-colored life he drew,
Exhausted worlds, and then imagined new:
Existence saw him spurn her bounded reign,
And panting Time toiled after him in vain.
  —Samuel Johnson
   (Prologue at the opening of Drury Lane Theatre, 1747)

Preface

I've been doing theater with young people from the ages of five to seventeen for the last twenty years and love it partly because I don't have to take it too seriously. For me, children's theater is a vehicle for group work that is fun. Adapting and modifying classical texts is part of the challenge. Plays are what the children make them and I enjoy writing scripts and rewriting plays based on my students' ideas as much as they enjoy the entire process of creating a performance.

My experience with theater has been integrated into my classroom and after-school work, in which I've modified plays I enjoy in order to suit the experience of theater to the concerns and joys of students.

This book, which emerged from my love of theater and from playing with dramatic forms, has five central notions:

• Plays are not sacred and can be adapted to suit the actors and the acting situation.

• Amateur theater done for pleasure should not bother with imitating professional productions, but should have as a goal the pleasure of the actors, their friends, and parents.

• Everyone who wants to play a role should have an opportunity to do so. Young people's theater should be non-competitive even if it means reconceiving and rewriting plays.

• Young playwrights should have an opportunity to have their work performed in workshops and communities without worrying about Broadway or even Off-Off-Broadway.

• Young people's theater can lead to a love of drama and help create an audience for those few people who are brave and obsessed enough to try to make playwriting and acting a career.

This book explores improvisation, reading and acting with scripts, adapting plays for young actors, and writing plays. The examples presented in the text are on various levels. Some are appropriate for young children between the ages of five and ten and others are more relevant to teenagers. Many can be modified and used with students of almost any age. In the bibliography, I have provided a list of resources so that a bit of reading and creative adaptation of texts can lead to an interesting drama program for just about anyone.

The chapters in this book are fairly independent of each other, so it's possible to jump into any chapter without having read the others. Many of the improvisations and scenes can be perused at leisure and integrated into your work in any order that fits what you are doing. I always begin with improvisations instead of a script, but there are other ways to work.

This book is for teachers with no particular experience or training in teaching theater, but who have a love of performance and enjoy a good play.

I'd like to thank all of the young people I've worked with over the years whose performances have given me at least as much pleasure as I hope they've experienced, including my own children Antonia, Erica, and Joshua, who have not only put up with the disorder of a house full of props, sets, and costumes, but acted in a number of our performances. I'd also like to thank Sande Zeig who has added a delightful element of comedy and mime to my perception of theater and has been wonderful to work with. The production of *The Four Alices and their Sister Susie in Wonderland* would never have happened without the creativity and enthusiasm of Deborah Ages and Susan Spurlock, whose contributions were essential. I also owe thanks to the band, Public Sector, and to Tom Rude and all of the other parents and people of Point Arena who have been so generous in supporting young people's theater. I also would like to thank Ron Padgett, Daniel Sklar, and Chris Edgar for their editorial sensitivity that has contributed a lot towards the final version of the book. Finally, I couldn't have done either theater or this book without the constant and creative support of my wife Judy, whose intelligence and judgement is woven throughout any decent work I've done.

Introduction
The Power of Illusion

Theater does not take place in real time and consists of creating convincing illusions of possible realities. The world of illusion is a very familiar and comfortable one for young people. Imagination — the free play of the mind with possible worlds, beings, and events—is easily engaged wherever children come together. For many children one of the saddest aspects of getting older is the closing down of the imagination as the price of fitting into adult-controlled worlds such as school and the so-called workplace. Too often, growing up means closing down.

This need not be the case. The imagination can and should be nurtured throughout life and the sense of play natural to childhood can be a continuing source of pleasure. We do not have to "grow up."

Theater is one source sustaining the life of the imagination. For many young people I have worked with, as well as for me, participating in the creation of theater is a source of joy and an escape from the dull routines that school too often represents. Improvisation, acting in classical or modern scenes and plays, and performing plays of one's own all engage the imagination.

Over the last twenty years, I have been playing around with theater in my classes. I had no training, I am not a good actor, and I can't memorize lines. Yet I love the stage, and decided when I was teaching in Berkeley in 1968 to try to teach drama. Seeing and reading plays and discovering Viola Spolin's *Improvisations for the Theater* were my only qualifications to teach drama. I taught in order to learn how to teach, and my students were wonderful about my fumbling attempts to teach what I was afraid I couldn't do.

1

One of the students in my first improvisation class, Phil Krauter (who was sixteen at the time), understood how tentative and insecure I was about teaching theater. When acting, he had an intensity and focus that sometimes scared me. There were times when I wasn't sure he was in control of himself, yet he always knew what he was doing with his face, voice, and body. Once we did an improvisation on going mad. Phil went mad, or at least I thought he had. He frothed and foamed and rolled on the floor, and then, like a paranoid, started threatening people. I insisted that all the other students leave the room, resolved to give up teaching improvisation, and set out to bring Phil back to reality. He was taller and stronger than I. I was afraid of him, but somehow my fear has always been tempered by my stubborn refusal to allow myself to be intimidated. I grabbed him and tried to shake him back to sanity. Phil just looked at me and laughed. He was in control all along. He had been acting, and told me that if I wanted to do serious theater I had to deal with serious actors.

Phil is involved in the theater professionally now, but most of the young actors, playwrights, set designers, and technicians I have worked with are not. Yet I hope that their experience with being a part of theater has given them a love for the stage, a continuing sense of playfulness, and an intelligence about performance that will provide lasting pleasure for them and create an audience for Phil's work and for the work of people who are seriously engaged in entertainment and education through performance.

The goals of doing theatre with young people are:

• to provide group experiences that break out of the competitiveness (and its tendency to isolate people) that dominates school life

• to learn to be part of an intelligent audience

• to learn how to speak well and control gesture and movement

• to introduce young people to classic and modern drama

• to learn how to create environments for performance

• to have fun being part of the illusory world of theater.

The fun of doing theater with young people is that, playing off the traditions of classic and contemporary theater, myth, fairy tale, and other literature, one can spin out new worlds and share them with others. First approaches to plays are magical. You start with young people who will not be who they are, with some characters, an empty stage, perhaps some props or costumes, and a story outline or theme, and then bring them together to the point where you are ready to share this created world with an audience. You can't tell what the final play will be like when you start out, and that uncertainty, coupled with the experience of living through the development of a performance, is an invaluable educational experience. Performance is not like filling out a workbook sheet or doing what an adult tells you. It emerges from within and from learning to become part of an ensemble. Consequently it provides a great opportunity for personal growth and for the development of group solidarity. And since the stage is illusion, it provides the rare opportunity for a shy child to take centerstage, a timid one to be brash, and a bully gentle. A number of students I've worked with have had severe stuttering problems, but on stage they speak and sing beautifully. In some cases, they were even able to transfer the confidence they developed through theater to their everyday speech. You never know what power and energy may emerge from a young person as soon as they step into character.

The Four Alices
and Their Sister Susie in Wonderland

Last year I did a production of *Alice in Wonderland* with five- to ten-year-old students at the Acorn School in Point Arena, California, where I was teaching. Actually it was a production of *The Four Alices and Their Sister Susie in Wonderland*, a country–western and blues version of *Alice* that owed its spirit and some of its story to Lewis Carroll.

Initially what I had in mind was a simple puppet show version of *Alice in Wonderland*, that had been read to the children during lunchtime over the course of several weeks. I made a very crude posterboard puppet of the Mock Turtle modelled on Thai stick puppets. There was a moveable hand and head and I played with it in class. The idea was to provide an accessible, easily constructed model of a character you could talk through. I thought the whole *Alice* puppet construction and show would take no more than an hour a day for a few weeks.

3

During free time and art class the kids made puppets — Alice after Alice after Alice with one March Hare, a few White Rabbits and an occasional Mock Turtle, Carpenter, Mad Hatter, Duchess, or Queen. As one of the girls explained to me, "After all there are so many Alices in the story that you can't make just one." She gave me three puppets: a tiny, tiny Alice, an Alice stretched large and out of proportion, and a regular-sized everyday Alice.

I didn't know what to do with all the puppets, and initially thought that we might end up with three or four troupes performing their own version of *Alice* for each other and possibly for the parents.

We did improvisations with the puppets. The idea was to become familiar with the puppet characters in different situations before reading Lewis Carroll's story and adapting scenes from it. It was a lot of fun to have many Alices talking to each other and to all of the other characters in ways that freed them from the structure of *Alice* and yet kept them within the spirit of Carroll's work.

During one of the improvisational sessions, a girl in the class said that the puppets were boring. She wanted to be Alice, not just play with an Alice puppet. Everyone in the class agreed and I realized that the play would have to move in this new direction.

I abandon my plans if students come up with more interesting and challenging ideas. There was no harm in trying to do a live *Alice in Wonderland* with the group. So, naively, I asked the children who would like to be Alice. There were five volunteers, one of whom dropped out and opted to be Alice's older sister. So it was up to me and Deborah, the co-teacher, as well as Susan, our aide and the music teacher, to decide who would be Alice. I begged off doing it on the spot and decided to think through the criteria for selection that night.

The more I thought about who should be Alice, the less I could choose and the less I wanted to. I had adapted classical plays for student performance before. In *A Midsummer Night's Dream*, I had twelve Pucks, and since most of six- and seven-year-olds wanted to be Puck, dividing up the role gave each of them an opportunity to speak a few lines of Shakespeare. Besides, Puck is everywhere, and in the spirit of Puck there was no reason why he couldn't have twelve faces. In *Macbeth* we had six or seven witches. After all,

4

what was one witch more or less to the spirit world? So why not four Alices? Any book that has magic mushrooms, talking rabbits, and an entire monarchy consisting of a deck of playing cards is perfect for fantasy and elaboration.

The next day in class I made the suggestion that we have four Alices. The kids were disappointed. They wanted to experience the competition between the four girls who wanted the role. However, I believe that education works best in the context of cooperation and joy, and I had no intention of yielding to their will. Children often pick up bad habits from the culture they are born into; besides, I have never felt obliged to perpetuate things that tear some children down and limit their aspirations.

So it was going to be four Alices and their older sister, but how could we do it in a way that would be convincing and exciting for the children? I discussed that problem with the whole group. We agreed that Alice, like any other person, has many aspects to her character, so there was no reason why four of the parts of Alice couldn't be on the stage at the same time. In other words, the children didn't want to take turns being Alice or split up the role. They all wanted to be fully Alice, and Susie wanted to have a part that was just as prominent as Alice's. I remember turning to the Alices and saying, "But which one of you is the real Alice?" They all raised their hands and shouted, "Me!"

At this point Susan Spurlock, the class aide and music teacher, started strumming on her guitar and someone in the room sang "Will the real Alice please stand up" and the girls responded, in song, "That's me." I suggested that Susan and the Alice s compose a song called "Will the Real Alice Please Stand Up." Here's what they came up with:

Will the Real Alice Please Stand Up
(Note: During this song the whole cast, with the exception of the Alices, sings everything but the words in quotation marks in the chorus parts. They are sung by the Alices.)

I'm so pretty
It's a pity
My neck's so long
From dusk to dawn

Chorus:
Will the real, real Alice
Please stand up.
"That's me."   That's who?
"That's me."   Uh huh.

Blond hair
Blue eyes
Can you tell me why
I grow so high

Chorus

My friend is mad
And he's so glad
The tea's not hot
And the mouse is in the pot

Chorus

What's the matter
With the Mad Hatter
Haven't you heard
He's crazy as a bird

Chorus

Why me
Can't you see
I'm so glad I'm Alice
In my palace

Chorus

A few days later the children, accompanied by Susan, sang the song and I realized we had moved from a simple puppet show to musical theater. I had to struggle with how far to take the play, how much time to spend on it, and where to fit it into what was already a very full educational program at the school. These problems are common when you are about to get carried away with doing theater and have other educational demands at the same time.

The first thing I decided, after talking with my colleagues, was that the play could not completely take over the work at the school, even though I was tempted to drop everything else and do *Alice*

6

exclusively. So to do the whole thing, I compromised and spent a half-hour to an hour a day for about three weeks, and then an hour or two a day for a week, and finally two full days before the performance. Fortunately Susan, our music teacher, and Deborah, my co-teacher, were willing to be part of the creative process. And we had parents, who, as the production developed, contributed generously to costumes, makeup, sets, and props.

Most teachers are not lucky enough to collaborate with other teachers. However, there are many ways in which similar situations can be created. Two classes, working together with parent volunteers and high school and junior high school students, can provide the backup needed to mount a major production, and one teacher and his students, with a few parent volunteers, can also do very fine children's theater. And plays performed in the classroom or for another class can be just as much fun as big productions. Theater can happen anywhere and on any scale and still be wonderful.

For me the central aspect of doing children's theater is to enjoy the fact that it is children's theater and not professional theater. It has to be fun, and need not lead to performance, though if it does, it should play for a friendly audience of children, parents, and other friends, as well as take advantage of the freedom of not having to aim for a move to Broadway. It exists for the sake of the children.

The Four Alices developed gradually and by sections. The White Rabbits worked up a comedy routine during recess; the Mad Hatter's tea party gained and then lost "guests." The Mad Hatter's version of "Twinkle, Twinkle, Little Star" was rewritten by Susan and the students and turned into a jazzy tune that the four Alices danced to in chorus-line style:

> Twinkle twinkle little bat
> How I wonder where you're at
> Up above the world so high
> Like a tea tray in the sky
>
> *Chorus:*
> Twinkle twinkle little bat
> How I wonder where you're at

Twinkle twinkle little rabbit
Why is being late your habit
You're always rushing here and there
But never getting anywhere

Chorus

Twinkle twinkle big fat queen
I wonder why you are so mean
You always scream "off with her head"
But if you do it, she'll be dead

Chorus

Twinkle twinkle Mister Hatter and hare
Teacups spilling everywhere
Everytime you drink you switch your cup
And then the dormouse fills it up

Chorus

Twinkle twinkle little Alice
We never see you in a palace
Wonderland, it is so strange
When you're there you always change

Chorus

The whole outline of the play developed slowly and digressively. There was simply too much in the book for us to use all of it on stage. Time constraints and the size of the class dictated that some things be eliminated and some be overemphasized. The overall outline was simple, too simple for some people, who wanted a finished script to work with from the start. Here is my working outline:

1. A narrator introduces the play and keeps it moving
2. The Alices and their sister Susie are on stage
3. White rabbits appear and do something
4. The Alices and Susie follow the rabbits into Wonderland
5. Bizarre things happen in Wonderland involving characters from the book and others the students might invent (one invented character at the Mad Hatter's tea party was called Dungeons and Dragons, a warrior who didn't know how to stop fighting and sat at the table stabbing and stabbing away at a tea biscuit, while shouting "Stagger, jabber, dagger, stagger, jagger. . . .")

8

6. The Alices and the whole cast end up at the Court and the Court scene ends with the Alices shouting, "You're nothing but a deck of cards."

7. The Alices return to the bank of the river and the unWonderland (the play almost ended this way but Susie didn't want to stay in the "real" world and so she provided the ending we used by saying, "It's boring here. I'm going back," and plunging down the rabbit hole a second time.)

The body of the play developed in sections, with the students picking their favorite parts. In this way everyone had great latitude of choice. In addition, all the sections of the play could be rehearsed independently (though the Alices and Susie had to rush around from group to group). That way parents and high school students could help fine-tune different sections of the work. I talked to our parent group and asked for help and patience.

For some of the adults and children, this piecemeal and improvisational approach to adaptation was frustrating. They wanted to know at any moment how the final product would look, but I didn't have the slightest idea. Part of helping people improvise plays is to encourage them to accept uncertainty and to realize that the whole endeavor is imaginative and fun; improvisational adaptation is a form of theme and variation on a classical play or story, or the development of an idea: it doesn't need to be predictable. Most of the children had little problem with that openness, but I had to work hard to convince the adults that a performance would emerge from our improvisations on *Alice in Wonderland.* However, I did provide structural diagrams of how the play looked as we progressed. Here is the final structure:

1. Overture and introduction by narrator.
2. Reality with the Alices and Susie.
3. The rabbits come on and do comic routine.
4. The Alices follow the rabbits.
5. Susie sings her song and then runs off after them to Wonderland.
6. They encounter the Caterpillar on a mushroom.
7. Then they encounter the Cheshire Cat and do Jabberwocky.
8. Then comes the Mad Hatter's tea party.

9. Then comes the Court at which the Mock Turtle leads "Won't you join the dance."
10. Then comes the confrontation between Alice and the Queen, Alice says "You're nothing but a deck of cards," and everyone throws cards into the air.
11. The Alices and Susie go back to reality.
12. Susie returns to Wonderland.

I created a script as we went along, improvising each scene over and over, exploring character, voice, and movement. At this point, I wanted the children to act rather than to memorize lines and recite them. Improvisation also provided alternatives on stage if students forgot the lines that they eventually were given. As it turned out, many lines were forgotten during the performances, but there was no panic and some of the best dialogue in the play emerged spontaneously when the actors were on the spot before an audience.

A week before the play, there were some children who still were not involved. By that time, the high school combo was rehearsing the songs with the kids and there was a need for sets and a tech crew. Some of the shy children were willing to do the tech work, and others had watched the rehearsals enough to decide how they would like to jump into the production. I've learned to add characters at the last minute and console children who find they can't deal with the pressures of performance, while redefining their roles to keep them in the process. There's always room on the tech and lighting crew, posters and programs must be made, and ushers might be needed. My goal was to involve everyone. If one of the children had not been engaged, the performance would have been empty for me.

We had one dress rehearsal, and spent two full school days dealing with the logistics of costumes, makeup, sets, props, etc. We did two performances, one for the school and one for the community. Then we had a cast party. The essential educational and emotional success of *The Four Alices* was not the quality of the performance, which I think was pretty good, but the fact that everyone played a part and knew that they made a contribution to the whole. See appendix A for script and lyrics to *The Four Alices*.

Chapter 1
Preparing to Do Theater

The actor is both the artist and the instrument—in other words the violinist and the violin. One could imagine what would happen if the violin or the piano started to talk back to the performer, complaining that it did not like to be struck in a certain way, that it did not respond to certain notes, that it was embarrassed at being touched sensually by a performer. This interaction between the artist and his instrument is precisely what transpires when the actor performs.
—Lee Strasberg

Beginning a drama program with a particular play in mind limits the range of what you can do with children in theater. It makes more sense to start with the students and their potential for creating imaginary characters and worlds, and for developing action and passion in the context of these created environments. This implies a lot of searching around at first, discovering who students are and how they perceive the culture and social world around them, as well as gaining insight into who they might like to pretend they are. This also means learning which themes are important to them, which events move, frighten, or amuse them. It means therefore, beginning with improvisation, conversation, props, costumes, themes, stories, and scenarios. It is important both to gather the essential resources for doing theater and to prepare students to do theater. And it is equally important to find a place to rehearse and to store props, costumes, and scenery.

The place can be as simple as a corner of the room defined by a rug or a small platform. It can be as grand as a high school auditorium. The storage space can be a costume/prop box, or a closet. It also might be an entire room in the basement of a school theater.

11

You begin with the unexpected, with the open-ended worlds that emerge through improvisation, and then you move towards the right play for the young people you are working with, the play that they feel is theirs and is good enough and exciting enough to share with an audience.

Improvisation

Doing theater with children consists of more than putting on plays. The performance of a play is a particular event, a focusing of talent and energy on a moment that happens and then passes. The development of the skills and sensibility that make for good theater also provides avenues for the development of self-confidence and sensitivity to the voices and gestures of others, and the experience of working collectively.

Because teaching drama has such serious potential, I like to start with charged themes, common but difficult emotions, gestures, and moments of discovery. Imagine the following:

You find yourself in front of a door in a strange house. You don't know how you got there, why you are there, or on what part of the planet the whole scene takes place. You are just there and have to open the door. How do you feel before touching the door knob? Express it in your face and body and then slowly reach for the knob while creating the room behind the door in your imagination. What happens?

This simple exercise bears repeating. On the first try with a group of children, there is often a monster behind the door, or something equally predictable. With repetition the imagination stretches a bit: you might find a book of spells, a key, a long passage, a sad or happy person, or another door behind the door. The more people become involved, the more it challenges everyone's imagination. Ideas lead to other ideas in the noncompetitive and nongraded world of free improvisation.

It's not difficult to invent situations that can lead to improvisation. Here are some to play with:

1. You fall asleep and then awake to find yourself on a strange planet. You hear footsteps approaching. What do you do?
2. There is a full moon and you are taking a walk admiring the sky when all of a sudden your skin feels funny. Little by little,

hair by hair, you find yourself transformed into a werewolf. Act out the transformation. Begin by seeing the moon and feeling very small changes in your hands, face, and feet.

3. You are escaping from prison and think you are being chased. Act out getting away. (This can also be done as an improvisation of running away from home.)

4. You find yourself, like Alice, transformed first into a tiny, tiny creature and then into a giant. Act out those changes and then "explain" your changes to a friend.

5. It is a stormy night and the electricity has gone off. You hear a strange noise in your house and go to discover what it is.

What these situations have in common is an element of mystery: a transformation, a discovery, or an uncertain outcome that challenges the improviser. All of them also have no single best way of being played. Good improvisational situations evoke multiple interpretations. They can also involve more than one person. It makes sense to do individual and group improvisations, and constantly to extend the boundaries of what your students do.

One way to come up with your own list of situations is to examine classical literature (including fairy tales and myths), much of which is full of mystery, challenges, uncertainty, and magic. For example, *The Tempest* begins with a shipwreck; Hamlet sees the ghost of his father and has to figure out whether he is dreaming or not; Little Red Riding Hood has to go through the dangerous woods; Hansel and Gretel plan to escape the witch; Orpheus has to descend into the underworld and, on returning to the land of the living, never turn to look back; Oedipus has to answer the riddle of the Sphinx. All of these themes can be transformed into improvisational situations.

The exercises as I've stated them so far are focused on unknown worlds in which the actor is still himself. Another basic method involves becoming someone who is not you: the actor has to learn to become another person and not to act every role as if the character were just a mirror of his own personality. This implies feeling what you don't feel, crying when you aren't sad, laughing when there's nothing to prompt laughter. Improvisation is preparation for the unnatural condition of becoming another person. It requires a control of emotion and gesture that is more accessible to young people than to adults. Kids fake it better, and in theater they can use all of the repertoire they have built up to deal with the adult world. Just ask a group of five-year-olds to pretend to cry or laugh and you'll experience the wild and wide range of children's emotional control.

Because improvisation warms children up for doing drama, I find it useful to begin every session with some warm–up exercises. These exercises change from group to group and often closely relate to the play we are doing. The children get to practice the emotions that are central to the play or to a play I would like to do with that particular group.

Improvisation is also a way I can read the students, find out what they would like to perform and what they are ready to do. There are times I don't tell students what play I would like to do until I see if they have the emotional range and psychological stamina the play demands. If the play isn't right for them, we switch to another one, because doing theater without enthusiasm can be as painful as being forced to study a subject you find boring and irrelevant. For years I've been wanting to do Samuel Beckett's *Waiting for Godot* and Clifford Odets' *Golden Boy* with young people, but have never found enough actors who wanted to do them. I still think of doing them but won't push my tastes and preferences on my students.

It is surprisingly simple to do improvisation with children, even if you have never done any theater before. Start with the simplest and most universal human activities and explore their variations. For example, one of my favorite activities for beginning improvisations is walking. There are thousands of ways to walk. First we clear an area for improvisation. Everyone sits against a wall facing the performance space. Then I ask for a volunteer to walk across the room. The first time we do this, most of the students are too shy to walk in front of everybody. An action that is easy, familiar, and thoroughly natural becomes awkward and a source of anxiety as soon as there is an audience. Usually, though, there are one or two children who are willing to get up. If not, I do it myself, walking slowly across the room. That is your basic walk, slow and as natural as possible when you know you are being watched.

The secret is to think of where you are going, not of the people watching you. One way to develop this type of mental concentration is to spend time thinking one's way into a situation before acting it out.

Walking is not usually random. One walks somewhere, through some environment, for some purpose. Young children can easily call up a destination, a scene, and a purpose, and when they do this they find it much easier to forget the audience and to act with grace and ease.

The simple walk is the beginning of one warm-up exercise. After a stroll across the room, here are some other ways of getting across the room:

- walking as if you're being followed
- walking when you're in a rush
- walking when you don't want to get where you're going
- walking through a snowstorm or hurricane
- walking across the desert or through a jungle
- walking when you're trying to keep up with someone who's walking faster than you can possibly walk
- walking and strutting in order to attract attention
- walking home after a wild party
- crawling and talking like a baby
- crawling and then taking your first step
- skipping
- jumping rope
- dancing to different tunes and thinking of someone you would like to be dancing with
- slipping on a banana

Each of these can be varied according to the environment and purposes children can imagine. Five minutes a day of walking warm-ups can set the scene for more complex theater. Some of my warm-up exercises begin with challenges such as these:

- You are 125 years old and have to walk up a mountain.
- You are walking home from school. It is your birthday and you know there will be a surprise party for you.
- You have a terrible report card and have to bring it home.
- It is raining and you are wearing a tee shirt. How do you walk home?

• You are late for your music lesson and you want to get there as quickly as possible.

A few seconds of meditation help get children in the mood to be in theatrical space. I use a traditional French theater convention to begin improvisation. Three knocks on the stage means that the play is about to begin. Give students several minutes to think themselves into an improvisation, and then, with a small hammer, knock three times, and they are out of their ordinary lives and into theater.

Falling is another fun exercise. There are as many ways to fall as to walk. Here are some: tripping; being tripped; parachuting; fainting; dying (there are many ways to die); stumbling like a baby and falling when you're learning to walk; jumping to the ground to duck something being thrown or shot at you; being hit; pretending you're going to fall and catching yourself so you recover and don't hit the ground; trying to prevent yourself from falling off a mountain or a tall building.

Falls can be done in slow motion, accompanied by sounds, exaggerated, and made comedic or tragic. There are several things to keep in mind when falling:

1. Where you are when you begin the fall.
2. Where you are falling to.
3. How the fall came about.
4. How you feel before the fall, while falling, and when you hit the ground.

Falls and walks come in handy in almost every play. They provide the beginnings of a theatrical repertoire that students can call on when they have to mold the characters they will become on stage.

It's fun to move from individual falls to group falls, to pantomimed murders, fights, chases, etc. Using mime and beginning with slow motion (which avoids a lot of the pain that falling can provide), it's great fun to have a whole class fall from the top of the Empire State Building, or pretend to die or collapse in laughter or tears.

Crying and laughing are much more difficult to control than walking. Before trying them, it makes sense to move from walking and falling to sitting, sleeping, and touching.

Touching another actor in the presence of an audience can be difficult for young people, especially if the person you have to touch is of the opposite sex or is not a friend. One approach to touch is through the relatively harmless act of handshaking. There are different ways to shake hands, and it is easy to work a handshake into a walking improvisation for two or more people. For example, people can walk in from different ends of the room and shake hands in the middle. The quality of the handshake is what makes that simple improvisation challenging. For example:

• Two people meet and shake hands warmly, with affection and delight.

• Two enemies meet, glare at each other and reluctantly shake hands.

• A child shakes hands with a very old person.

• Two boxers shake hands and go to their corners ready to come out fighting.

• A hand-shaking maniac runs around the room shaking everybody's hand.

• A group stands around in a circle. Everybody tries to shake everybody else's hands.

• Try shaking left hands instead of right hands.

After handshaking, one can move on to bumping, embracing, walking hand in hand, and other forms of physical contact. One thing I have avoided has been kissing, which, whenever I suggested it, has been thoroughly rejected by my students, except as highly formal kissing in the context of a performance of a play.

From movement it makes sense to add voice. Screaming or shouting is one way to begin unless you are worried about what the teacher next door might say. For most young people, screaming, like any use of the voice in improvisation and on stage, is more difficult than using the body. Yet it is a good way to begin to integrate movement and voice.

Improvising a scream and a fall, a crowd at a ball game, or an encounter with a monster are a few ways to get the voice going. It probably is best to build voice onto and into action. From screams it is possible to get to cries, laughs, and eventually felt speech.

Stage crying is not easy unless you have something in mind to cry about. In fact learning to cry when you're not unhappy is a complicated exercise in self-control. I remember trying to get some of the Alices to cry because they were so far from home and in such a mad world. Every time an Alice almost managed tears she burst out laughing. We spent days on crying until T'ai, one of the Alices, said she was ready to do it. T'ai has a radiant, smiling face and I'd never seen her cry. She asked for a stool and sat down in front of the group. Then slowly she cupped her hands around her face and bent over. She slowly lifted her head towards us and took her hands away. There were tears rolling down her face.

Afterwards she explained that she made herself remember something terrible that made her cry when she was three. We all worried about her and she watched our faces and then smiled and told us it was just theater. Without knowing it, T'ai had discovered the technique of using "emotion memory," the emotional re-creation of strong past experiences to enhance the emotional power and truth of acting, described by Konstantin Stanislavsky in *An Actor Prepares*. Stanislavsky describes this technique, which is very powerful for developing emotional content in improvisations:

The type of memory, which makes you relive the sensations you once felt. . .is what we call 'emotion memory.' Just as your visual memory can reconstruct a visual image of some forgotten thing, place or person, your emotional memory can bring back feelings you have already experienced. They may seem to be beyond recall, when suddenly a suggestion, a thought, a familiar object, will bring them back in full force.

According to Stanislavsky, this emotion memory makes it possible for actors to learn how to express genuine emotion on stage and not merely to imitate emotion. Children are particularly open to the expression of feeling and to transferring it to the fictional world of the stage, and Stanislavsky's ideas about acting work well with children, who are natural method actors.

T'ai's example became a model for the other children. They used their memory of other situations in order to produce the emotion needed in a particular dramatic context.

Another way to encourage the development of voice is the use of props. A telephone, a chair, a mirror, a street sign, a table, or several chairs and place settings, flashlights, a walkman, glasses and liquor bottles filled with colored water, a wallet filled with play money, suitcases and their contents, all these can lead to dozens of improvisations.

For example, with a telephone you can:

- get a call telling you that you've won a million dollars
- make a call telling someone that their pet has been run over
- make a call to a friend and gossip about another friend who then enters the room
- talk while your mother or father is screaming at you to get off the phone
- talk to your date while your brother or sister is listening on the extension.

A street sign can set a scene in which:

- you're waiting for someone who doesn't show up
- you're lost in a strange city
- you bump into someone who's coming around the corner
- you're waiting for someone who arrives just as you are about to leave
- you meet someone who hands you some stolen goods
- you're meeting a spy from another country to pass government secrets. (Variations on this: the spy shows up and then a government agent catches you; you mistake a stranger for the spy; or you are a police officer and have set the spy up.)

After doing a number of improvisations with props, a good exercise is to have groups of students pick a prop and have them make up improvisations for other students to do. Each group can set the scene for their improvs and give the instructions. For students, this is a good first experience in directing.

There are many other ways to experiment with improvisation. Sometimes it makes sense to do it as you are developing a play. Other times improvisation is fun in itself. The basics of walking, running, sitting, laughing, crying, etc. can lead to the more complex imitation of panic, fright, love, infatuation, defiance, anger, and malevolence.

The Use of Significant Themes in Improvisation and in the Development of Plays

When moving from simple improvisations to complex scenes, it is useful to brainstorm with your students about issues and encounters that intrigue, amuse, frighten, or excite them. Recently I did a workshop with elementary and secondary school teachers who were interested in doing drama with their classes. I had them make a list of themes that they felt their students would be interested in exploring through improvisation.

Some of the themes we came up with were: personal loss, rites of passage, the struggle for personal independence, the generation gap, eating and eating problems (from being overweight to bulimia and anorexia), family strife, going to war or resisting war, first love, impossible love, witchcraft, race, rejection, dignity and self-esteem, the clown and the fool, messing up and being awkward, imaginary friends and worlds, making and losing friends, teachers and mentors, genius and talent, hearing your inner voice, crime and the character of the criminal, the masks people wear, childhood's end, eccentricity and madness, being funny, problems of identity and self-acceptance, historical moments and the passage of time, prettiness and ugliness (the beauty and beast syndrome).

Here's how three of these themes can be elaborated on through improvisation and worked into play form or used to prepare students to perform published plays.

(But let me digress for a moment. In developing improvisations, many acting teachers make a distinction between situational improvisations and "results"-oriented improvisations. The situational improv is one that begins with a situation, and the results-oriented one begins with a particular feeling. For example, "You wake up after having a sad dream" is situational, whereas "You wake up feeling sad" implies result. In the first case, many different feelings—relief, fear, anxiety, sadness, or indifference—might ensue. In the second, "sadness" is the only emotion to be portrayed. Professional acting teachers prefer situational improvs; some teachers feel that results improvs should be avoided altogether. I've found that both work well with children. There are times when I simply ask students to laugh, cry, or pretend to sulk, thus making them create their own situations. Other times I give them a situation and have them decide its emotional content. For me, the role of improvisation is to build up a repertoire of responses and an ability to respond quickly and spontaneously to a given theme or idea or situation.

When you think through a theme, you're left with more ideas than can ever be realized in a classroom. Choose a theme, play with it yourself, and then decide where, with all of the possibilities available, you want to jump in with your students.)

The first of the three themes is appropriate for children of any age: Making Friends and Losing Friends. Everyone longs for a friend or two or more, and just about everyone loses friends, tries unsuccessfully to have someone be a friend, and is jealous of other people's friends.

Friendship has its problems as well as its rewards. How loyal should one be to a friend in trouble? What do you do if your friend wants to steal your lover? How do you react if your friend insists that you can't have any other friends? What happens to friendship when you have to leave home for a job or for college? What happens when you and your closest friend are slowly drifting apart? What is a reunion with a friend you haven't seen for years like? How does it feel to have no friends or to have friends who you feel are suffocating your life? When do certain friends become burdens and what do you do when that happens?

These are only a few aspects of friendship. But there is a point at which one has to stop spinning out ideas and jump in and do something with the kids. Here are a few ways to begin improvisations relating to friendship.

1. *For Two People:* Each person feels that he or she has never had a friend and is incapable of making close friendships, yet both long for that closeness. They meet somehow (waiting at a bus stop, in a cafe—anywhere that strangers might meet) and have a chance to get to know each other. What do they do?

2. *For Three People:* Two of the three are best friends. The third person wants to break up that relationship, and either be one of their best friends or a very good friend of both of them. Begin with the two friends and then have the third person enter.

3. *For Two People:* Two people are best friends. One was born with a handicap that people make fun of. Create a conversation between these two people in which one tries to assure the other of his love and support after a particularly bad insult has taken place.

Three-Person Variant: Two people, one of whom is handicapped, walk down the street. A third person comes up and acts in an insulting manner. What happens?

4. Two old friends meet after not having seen each other for twenty-five years. Improvise what they talk about and try to recreate twenty-five years of experience, some of which you might like to share with your friend and some of which you wish to keep hidden (though it might sneak out in your conversation).

5. A friendship or love relationship is breaking up. How many different ways can this be done? Do a series of "breaking up is hard to do" improvisations.

All five of these improvisational situations can be done for the pleasure of exploring the phenomena of friendship. They can also be tied into plays you might want to do with your students. For example, the first improvisation can lead into a production of *Bus Stop*, an adaptation of *Rebel without a Cause*, or any other play or story that deals with the theme of longing for a friend.

The second one can lead students into working on plays or adaptations of movies and stories dealing with jealousy and unrequited or impossible love. Anton Chekhov, Eugene O'Neill, and Federico Garcia Lorca are some of the many authors one can turn to.

The third improvisation is an invitation to do *Of Mice and Men* or to adapt Ron Jones' *Say Ray* or *The Acorn People*. The fourth is central to the theme of a play like *The Women*, and to movies like *The Big Chill* and *Same Time Next Year*. It is a good way of getting young people to fantasize about the future and create their own plays and scenes.

There is no end to break-ups in the theater and on film. Some classics are *Casablanca, Hamlet* (the scenes between Hamlet and Ophelia can lead to wonderful improvisations), *He Knew What He Wanted* (known in its musical version as *The Most Happy Fellow*), *Picnic*, and *Romeo and Juliet*.

A second theme interesting to experiment with is Personal Loss. This can range from losing your favorite teddy bear to experiencing the death of someone you love. The following situations can lead to improvisations that introduce the theme. The first three are appropriate for elementary school students, and the next four for junior and senior high school students. The same theme has to be explored in different contexts and on different levels of complexity for different age groups.

- You are walking down the street and find a stuffed bear in a garbage can. You look around, take the bear and talk to it, reassuring it that you will take it home, care for it, and never throw it out.

- Your family is moving and you are told that you can't take all of your stuffed animals. How do you tell your animals that you're taking some and leaving others? What do you do with the ones left behind?

- Your pet rat has just died and you are taking it out to bury it. How do you say farewell?

- (Perhaps best for older students.) You discover that you have cancer or AIDS. What do you say to your family? (This can be extended to a second scene in which others discover you are about to die and discuss your imminent death. Then you walk into the room.)

- There are two people on stage, one a ruler and one an assassin. The assassin reflects on the problems of killing, the ruler on the fear of being killed.

- Children return from the funeral of their parents who have died in an accident. What do they say to each other?

- You have lost your wallet with all of your ID and money in a strange town. You have to catch a plane and need twenty dollars to get to the airport. A number of strangers walk back and forth across the stage. How do you approach them?

My favorite way to introduce the subject of loss is to use the final scene of *Hamlet*. It's a way of getting young children to speak a few lines of Shakespeare and feel part of a grand theatrical tradition. I begin with a rather casual version of the plot, explaining that there's this young guy just home from school who's out walking in the fog. He's depressed because his father has died and his mother has remarried. It just so happens that he's a prince and his mother and stepfather are the king and queen of Denmark. All of a sudden Hamlet sees his father's ghost, who reveals that he was murdered by Hamlet's stepfather, who is now shacked up with the queen and is casting a bloody shadow over all of Denmark. The ghost tells Hamlet to kill the usurper, but to be sure to leave Gertrude (Hamlet's mother and the queen) alone. Now imagine what goes on in Hamlet's mind. Is the ghost just an illusion, or actually the restless spirit of Hamlet's father telling the truth? Is Hamlet so upset by the death of his father that he is going crazy?

At this point the improvisations begin. What does Hamlet tell himself, how does he feel, what will he do? (There is no reason why Hamlet can't be made into a princess, so female students can do the improvisations.)

How is the loss of a father and the call for revenge experienced? How do you find out the truth? What tricks do you use to get the new king to give himself away? These themes form the substance of the play, but there is only so much one can do in a few improvisation sessions. So I jump to the final scene. Hamlet is challenged by his stepfather, the king, to have a duel with Laertes, the brother of Ophelia and the son of Polonius. In the course of the play, Ophelia, who was in love with Hamlet, has committed suicide. Polonius was accidentally killed by Hamlet, who mistook him for the king, his stepfather. Shakespeare revelled in complex family relationships.

From Laertes' point of view, his duel with Hamlet is an act of revenge. From the king's perspective it is a convenient way to get rid of Hamlet. The king puts poison on the tip of Laertes' sword and in the cup of wine that Hamlet will drink if, by chance, he happens to kill Laertes and does not get wounded himself. As I like to tell my students, the king wasn't taking any chances. Hamlet knew too much and had to go.

(By the way, Leon Garfield's *Shakespeare's Stories* is the best retelling of Shakespeare's plays I have found. The book is supposed to be for young people, but it's interesting for anyone who would like to read a clear, elegant exposition of twelve of Shakespeare's most familiar plays.)

With my students, the duel, the death of Hamlet, and the sorrow of Horatio are the subjects of the improvisation. First of all, we improvise dying. There are slow ways to die, fast ways to die, dramatic and tragic ways to die, and funny ways to die. Since most children have seen a lot of movies and TV, they have witnessed (though not necessarily experienced) a lot of dying. So we do death improvisations:

- Say farewell to your family and die.
- Die as you are being tortured.

- Pretend you are dying and then show you were only fooling.
- Die from a knife wound.
- Die from a bullet wound.
- You are walking along and something falls out of the sky and kills you totally unexpectedly.

Then we do two-person improvs. One of the children is a corpse, the other a murdered or a mourner. I look for the right moment to introduce a word I learned from young actors in London, "corpsing." Corpsing is the worst thing you can do on stage. "To corpse" is to turn the character you are playing into a dead body; to fall out of character and relax or laugh or forget that you are on stage, even for a second. I prefer "corpsing" to its American counterpart, "breaking character."

I use the concept of corpsing as a way of reminding my students that they are on stage during an improvisation, even if the "stage" is a corner of the classroom and the audience is just a few friends. "You're corpsing!" is my form of negative evaluation. As long as they stay in character, students are free to play any role in the way they choose. Of course, this means they have to think a bit about how they will create, on stage, someone who is not them.

Once we have done improvisations of dying and mourning from Hamlet, I introduce Shakespeare:

> Now cracks a noble heart. Good night sweet prince,
> And flights of angels sing thee to thy rest!

I ask everybody to memorize those two lines and then we render them in class in dozens of ways: with deep dramatic sadness, with inner sorrow, with cynicism, with mirth, with religious fervor, with boredom, etc.

Then we put the pieces together: one child is the dying Hamlet and the other is Horatio. Hamlet chooses how to die and Horatio chooses how to mourn. Only the scene and the words are constant.

There are many other plays that embody the theme of personal loss and they range from tragic to comic. There is loss in *Arsenic and Old Lace* just as much as there is in *King Lear*. The important thing for young people is to get a feel for what a play is about—what the central themes and emotions are, and how they are being treated by the playwright — rather than to memorize the lines or know the names of the authors or characters.

Take the theme of eating. What can be done with it through improvisation and how can it lead to the performance and writing of plays? Here are a few suggestions:

- Everyone in the room has a cone of their favorite ice cream. Pretend that you are eating the cone to the last little tasty bit.

- Two people go out to dinner. They have been going out together for several years and one of the two is fed up. In fact, that person has someone else they are seeing on the sly. This is the break-up dinner. What happens?

- Two people go out to dinner. One proposes marriage, but the other isn't so sure about getting married at this stage.

- Food makes one of the actors sick. He knows it's stupid and unhealthy, but he just can't eat. The rest of the family is worried and tries to convince him to eat. (The family can be large or small. There can be several scenes with mother and child; father and child; mother, father, and child; sister and child; etc.)

- A table is set but there is no food. In fact, no food ever comes. What do the people around the table do?

Although these just touch the surface of what can be done with the theme of food and the rituals of eating, they are examples of how a very simple activity can lead to complex improvisations.

Some Specifics on Selecting and Developing Themes

According to John Howard Lawson, in his book *Theory and Technique of Playwriting*:

The essential character of drama is social conflict in which the conscious will is exerted: persons are pitted against other persons, or individuals against groups, or groups against other groups, or individuals or groups against social or natural forces.

The conflicts that Lawson refers to can be comic or tragic; they can be set in situation comedies, mysteries, or melodramas. Tension and imbalance, however, are what engage the imagination of the actor and the attention of the audience. When developing themes for improvisations, look for the tensions, oppositions, and resolutions of conflict that can be dramatized. Below is a grab bag of ideas, situations, and settings you might begin with. Each of them can be treated in many different ways and therefore can be returned to over and over again. I like to select a theme or situation, divide my class into a number of small groups, then ask each group to develop improvisations around that theme or situation and to perform them for each other. After the performances, we usually discuss the different treatments we've explored and talk about other ways to approach the same subject.

Here are some situations for improvisation:

- Running away from home
- A love triangle, with two people loving a third person who may or may not love either of them
- Jealousy over wealth or love
- Greed and envy
- Snobbery
- Power struggles over control of a family, nation, or planet, or struggles with one's own madness
- A plane that is about to crash
- The outbreak of war
- A sinking ship
- A fire
- An earthquake or avalanche
- A slippery surface such as a waxed floor or a frozen lake or patch of ice
- A crowded restaurant where any waiter might spill a tray on some of the customers
- A shopping trip where people end up with more packages than they can carry
- A dark room where people keep bumping into each other
- A street with potholes and cracks.

Here are some other suggestions for developing themes:

1. Affection, infatuation, and love lend themselves to improvisation. However, love is a difficult theme to develop with young people. They are not shy about real love, but very reticent when it comes to pretending on stage to love someone. It's probably best to begin with affection, toward siblings and pets for instance, and

27

then ease toward love relationships. Some situations that have worked for me are:

- Someone is picking on your younger brother or sister. What do you do?
- You bring home a puppy or kitten and have to persuade your mother or father to keep it.
- Two people who have been going out for a while are sitting on a bench in the park. One proposes marriage.
- Someone is dying and others try to tell that person how much they love her or him.
- There is a family reunion and people reminisce about their childhood together and their loves and hates.

2. Fantastical transformations present rich occasions for the development of theatrical skills. Here are some ways to begin focusing on transformations:

- Everyone in the group lies down and thinks his or her way into some character with magical powers. Then other people have to figure out what those powers are by interacting with the group.
- Make up a list of characters or personality types and write them down on separate cards. Students pick a card at random and act out the character they have picked. Fast changes of personality are also possible.
- Let everyone become the monster of his or her choice by showing how the transformation from the everyday self to the monster takes place, step by step.
- One student approaches a door, behind which another student has been transformed into a magical creature of some kind. What happens when the door is opened?
- Some ugly but kind creatures land on Earth. How do they convince people that their appearance is just an earthling's interpretation of ugliness and threat and that they want to be friends?

When you attempt to turn themes for improvisation like the ones illustrated into specific improvs, there are several ways to make the transition from idea to performance easy:

- Create specific details.
- Introduce a few props.
- Set the scene.
- Give everyone time to prepare privately or in small groups.

• Develop a ritual for focusing student attention and getting them ready to act. The ritual eliminates giggling, nervousness, and all of the little ceremonies of self-consciousness that precede performance. The ritual I use is knocking three times with a hammer or mallet on a hard surface. It is also possible to ring a bell or buzzer, clap your hands, or flick the lights. This focuses the actors and the rehearsal audience on the fact that theater time has begun and therefore the "real" world should be abandoned for a while. It is illusion time.

Here are some examples of how to use props and stagecraft in improvisations to develop a theater environment:

• Improvisations on the theme of running away from home benefit from simple props like a suitcase and some clothes to pack or even something as simple as a toothbrush to put in your pocket. They also profit from setting a scene that might range from an argument with your parents about going out with someone they refuse to let you see, to wanting to get away from the battles your parents have with each other. Sometimes it even helps to make up names for the characters in an improvisation or to ask students to think themselves into characters with those names.

• Improvisations based on the theme of being on a sinking ship can be set with props as simple as a table with several chairs and place settings. As the ship goes down, the table tips—the actors can invent ways to undermine the table. Other props might be a box of jewels, a briefcase full of important papers, or any other form of valuable that can be lost or destroyed. Or you could have one life jacket and five people. The prop becomes the focus for the development of emotion and the flow of events. You might also create a name for the ship, a destination, a picture of the hopes and dreams of the voyagers, or even a detailed account of the moments before the ship crashes.

• Props are particularly important when doing comedy. A restaurant scene is enhanced by a tray and a glass of water to carry on it; a scene of slipping on the ice is helped along by having some packages to carry. It's also fun to try to move furniture around in a dark room.

• Improvisations on themes of affection are helped by simple details. A pet can be represented by a basket with a blanket sticking out of it; death can be put in front of the class by having one student lying on the floor covered with a sheet.

• Fantastical themes are often played well in strange lighting. Colored gels over the lights in a room, flashlights, lamps lying on the ground and facing up, all create an ambience of mystery. Within that context, young people can create their own improvisations.

Chapter 2
Developing a Performance

Players and painted stage took all my love,
And not those things that they were emblems of.
—William Butler Yeats

Improvisation sets the groundwork for doing plays. The thematic approach to improvisation I've been describing can be used in several ways. One way is to learn from the improvs which themes your students find most compelling, and work with those themes to develop plays out of the improvisations. You can also introduce selections from plays and stories that treat the same themes.

Students' interests vary considerably. Some groups love fantasy, while others want to deal with conflict in the adult world. Some like adventure and others romance or catastrophe. Five- to seven-year-olds usually love fantasy and fairy tales, but sometimes a group of high school students will take a fancy to a fairy tale and want to do something more than improvisation with it.

Some of my high school students decided to stage *Snow White and the Seven Dwarfs* for a local elementary school. We had done improvisations on children's relationships to their stepparents, wicked and otherwise, and had been discussing Norma Klein's *Mom, the Wolf Man and Me*, which is about the tension that develops when a single parent falls in love and has to deal with her child's jealousy. The wolf man of the title was the equivalent of Snow White's wicked stepmother.

At the same time that we were doing the improvisations, the students were studying the structure and horrible effects of apartheid. We began to develop *Snow White* through improvisations, and we read Lore Segal's translation of the Grimm tale that was published in *The Juniper Tree* (this two-volume set belongs in every teacher's personal library and classroom).

When we came to the Seven Dwarfs some unexpected improvisations developed. The first thing the students noted was that the dwarfs were all men, living alone in a house with no women in their lives. Some students said that it sounded like the diamond and coal mine dormitories in South Africa, where miners are not allowed to live with their families. The students decided to render the dwarfs as oppressed coal miners and Snow White as a white liberal who was trying to help them overthrow the reign of the wicked apartheid government of South Africa. From there a whole new version of *Snow White* developed, with the focus on the dwarfs and political struggle. We performed this adaptation of *Snow White* for ourselves and several friends, as it didn't seem appropriate for the kindergartners and first graders for whom we had originally intended it. It was also something that the students felt the community wasn't ready for. In this case, as in many others I've experienced, the students expressed opinions much more conservative than my own. But, as I've had to teach myself to do, I went along with what they felt were acceptable and unacceptable risks. I told them what my feelings were, but because the students were taking the risks and I wasn't, *Snow White and the Seven Exploited Miners* became a private performance.

Another time, when I was doing improvisations on the theme of getting lost with five- to eight-year-olds, I brought in a copy of the stage adaptation of James Thurber's fable, *The Little Girl and the Wolf*, a rendering of Little Red Riding Hood. It was part of the play *A Thurber Carnival*.

The Little Girl and the Wolf
The MUSIC begins, the theme is childlike and rollicking. The SPOTLIGHT picks out the NARRATOR, played by the FIRST WOMAN. She is seated Right of Center on the edge of the platform stage, wearing her evening costume. The TRAVELLER opens revealing all three tree panels in place, giving the impression of a Thurber forest. The light is soft Upstage and bright Downstage.
NARRATOR: One afternoon a big wolf waited in a dark forest for a little girl to come along carrying a basket of food to her grandmother. (WOLF, played by SECOND MAN, and wearing a leather motorcycling jacket and cap, enters from behind the Left second portal. He crosses to Center, and paces Right and Left looking for a little girl. He

32

stops Center.) Finally a little girl did come along and she was carrying a basket of food.

(LITTLE GIRL, played by THIRD WOMAN, is wearing a very short red dress. It has a ruffle around the bottom of the skirt which ends just above the knees in front but swoops up shorter in the back revealing her lovely black stockinged legs. She also wears high heeled black pumps and carries a small straw basket bag, lined in red. She walks with small mincing steps in time to the music. She enters from Down Left; crosses Right to Center where the WOLF suddenly turns to face her and block her path.)

WOLF: Are you carrying that basket to your grandmother?

NARRATOR: asked the wolf. The little girl said

LITTLE GIRL: Yes, I am.

NARRATOR: So the wolf asked her

WOLF: Where does your grandmother live?

NARRATOR: and the little girl told him *(LITTLE GIRL points Off Right. The WOLF sights along her arm, then, standing behind her, taps her left shoulder. As the LITTLE GIRL looks Left, the WOLF turns and crosses Upstage and through the Center revolve which has partially opened. When the WOLF has passed through, it closes behind him.)* and he disappeared into the wood. *(The LITTLE GIRL discovers the WOLF's trick, shrugs, and takes tiny steps Upstage Center, to her grandmother's house.)* When the little girl opened the door of her grandmother's house *(LITTLE GIRL mimes opening a door, and the RIGHT REVOLVE turns in with the WOLF. He wears a ruffled lace nightcap and is sitting behind a cut-out bed.)* she saw that there was somebody in bed with a nightcap and nightgown on. She had approached no nearer than twenty-five feet from the bed *(LITTLE GIRL measures the distance from the bed; too far, she takes two steps right. The WOLF beckons her nearer.)* when she saw that it was not her grandmother but the wolf *(LITTLE GIRL steps back.)* for even in a nightcap a wolf does not look any more like your grandmother than the Metro-Goldwyn lion looks like Calvin Coolidge. So the little girl took an automatic out of her basket and shot the wolf dead. *(LITTLE GIRL takes an automatic out of her basket, aims, and shoots the WOLF in the head. He slumps over Right.)* Moral:

WOLF: *(Sits up straight.)* It is not so easy to fool little girls nowadays as it used to be. *(Falls back, dead.)*

BLACKOUT

(The MUSIC concludes with a cool flourish, the TRAVELLER closes.)

The children thought the ending was hilarious and wanted to do their own version of *Little Red*. Two boys and a girl wanted to be Riding Hood, only they decided they wanted to be Little Lead Riding Hood, a gangster; Big Red, another gangster; and Hood Red Riding, an alien from outer space. The wolf was to be a radiation monster who was a notorious polluter of the environment (environmental issues, especially coastal oil development, are very important in our community). The short play that developed was performed for parents and other students, along with a number of other student-created plays. The play was an environmental fairy tale ending with the alien and the three Reds finding a way to neutralize the wolf's radioactivity and decontaminate Grandma.

With older students it is possible to mix playwriting with improvisation. I like to begin by discussing some general aspects of the structure of plays, and then move quickly to having students write and deliver monologues. Here are five general principles we discuss (there are of course exceptions to them, especially in experimental theater):

1. Every play is out of real time and action.

Eating a stage meal does not take as long as eating a meal; stage fights do not produce injury, death, or even real blood; stage kings do not give up ruling actual kingdoms; and stage love does not imply genuine affection. This might seem obvious, but many beginning young actors and playwrights don't seem to know it. I've seen meal improvisations and stage fights that went on and on beyond any theatrical usefulness or interest and read dozens of dinner scenes that were interminable because the students had a real meal and not a theatrical purpose in mind. What the children had in mind was eating and fighting, not placing eating and fighting on stage.

Many students won't play romantic roles on stage because they are afraid it implies real love. And I've seen children take the loss of an imaginary kingdom very seriously, even to the point of refusing to hand over their crowns during a rehearsal or performance and refusing to die on stage long after their character was already dead.

The difference between stage reality and life must be emphasized continuously. This can be done through the improvisation of very simple activities. For example, students try to act out a meal in real time, including all the waiting for the serving of food and clearing of dishes. They try to recreate every bite of the specific menu chosen for the improvisation. It is a very frustrating experience and one that leads to the idea of eliminating irrelevant motion and activity, of condensing the life moment into a theater moment, and of pretending to do something ordinary rather than actually doing it.

Then the activity can be sped up and the players focused on dialogue and emotion, not the food.

At this point you can transfer the improvisation to a performance context and point out that the curtain can open or close (or the lights go up or fade out on an open stage) at any time during the action. This makes for an occasion to develop a scene, the basic unit of play construction.

Here are some simple examples of how improvisations can lead to scenes:

• The improvisation opens in the middle of the meal. As the main course is being served, one of the characters points to another and says: "Will you marry me?" Or says any of the following: "I'm leaving you." "I got my draft notice." "They want me to leave tomorrow." "I have some very bad news."

• The improvisation takes place in a beauty parlor (hair cutting salon). One person is setting another's hair. Several people sit waiting. The hairdresser begins to gossip about one person in the room until that person gets upset and leaves. Begin in the middle of the conversation, end at the right dramatic moment.

• Two people are about to have a fight. A third person breaks it up. It's the job of the students who are not in the improvisation to decide when and how to begin and end the scene.

• People are waiting at a bus stop. The bus never comes. How do you make a scene out of the wait? How does it begin, how do you end before all the actors are bored?

2. *Plays are meant to be performed before an audience.*

It is important to think about how you want the audience to feel and what you want them to see when you do theater. It's hard for children to learn how to show their bodies and faces and how to project their voices without shouting. For that reason, improvisations (especially on a stage) should be observed by other students who pay attention to the actors' bodies, faces, and voices. It is the audience's role to critique the others in specific ways and play the role of director.

Everyone should have a chance to direct. (Some students, however, don't like directing, especially if the children they are to direct are not their friends and deliberately refuse to listen to them. There is no point in forcing anyone to direct.) Watching a student direct other students can be a powerful experience. Here are some techniques that can be used to help the fledgling director.

I walk around the stage or playing area while the young directors watch from the audience. I deliberately mess up by mumbling, turning my back to the audience, corpsing, walking awkwardly across stage, and then ask them to tell me what to do to make what is happening on stage more convincing.

Next, ask young directors to move about the stage and act in the worst ways they can imagine. This is an attempt to focus attention on what might go wrong when you try to direct other students.

After sensitizing students to stage embarrassment, I try to help them understand that their role is to create good theater, not humiliate others. That means doing things like suggesting that a walk or speech or handshake might be performed more effectively, rather than dwelling on how terrible the first attempt was. It is essential in young people's theater to concentrate on how to do things better rather than to criticize what went wrong.

I also suggest ways of gently halting a scene and starting it all over again. A simple phrase such as "Take it from the top" can be used as a sign that things aren't going well and that everybody should take a deep breath and start all over again. This technique shows trust for the actors' intelligence. It also gives young directors a sense of how much can be rehearsed in one session, how far actors can be pushed, and how the weak parts of a production can be detected before public performance.

It's a good idea to have young directors study the psychological, social, cultural, and class roles of the characters in the plays they are working with and to have them keep a director's notebook with sketchy notes of character analysis, plot development, and suggestions for staging.

I encourage young directors to develop improvisations that develop these characters. I encourage students to elaborate on the improvisations we have done together and to create wholly new ones that might represent moments in the lives of their characters or in the context of the story they are telling on stage.

Young directors should be given the opportunity to modify the script or scenario and add or subtract scenes or characters according to what they feel will make a better play.

Finally, it is essential to sit in the back of the room or theater when a young person is directing for the first time. Encourage him or her to ask for help when there's trouble, and to talk frequently about the progress of the work. (A bit of advice: give your suggestions in private, or you will be undermining the work of the student director.)

It is also invaluable to take advantage of every opportunity to see live performances with your students and get them accustomed to talking about what they have seen. Amateur community theater, professional productions of mainstream plays, avant-garde plays, and acting classes at local colleges and high schools all create a theatrical literacy that can be transformed into sensitive on-stage performance, and also lead to a love of drama.

I've found that even in the most remote or unlikely places, there is some high school or community theater whose actors are flattered to show off their work to young people, and to let them attend rehearsals as well as performances.

If, however, there is no theater available for your students, there are lots of plays and film adaptations of plays that are available on video. These can expose students to extraordinary acting and help them understand play structure.

3. Plays turn on action.

The action in plays can be physical, mental, or spiritual, but something has to happen in the course of the performance. Many beginning improvisations by students consist of unending fights, conversations without point, and jokes and comic acts that only the actors understand.

Play structure develops slowly. There is nothing wrong with pure fun and the development of ease before an audience of friends.

But there's more to theater. After a while it's important to add elements of structure and content. For example, a simple improvisation of a fight that has no predetermined structure can raise the following issues:

- Who are the combatants? Are they friends or enemies?
- What historical period are they living in?
- How would the fight look in slow motion?
- Should we improvise the events that led up to the fight?
- Should we just do the first few blows, and skip to the end of the fight?
- Should we improvise what happened to the fighters after the fight was over? What did they do? How did they feel?
- Now put it all together knowing that you not only have to end the fight but keep the improvisation going into the postfight activities.

Have your students think of the before and after of the scene too, as they go from simple improvisations to the development of scenes and whole plays.

4. Plays have to establish themselves in specific places, real or imaginary.

Students should learn, on the microlevel, how to cross rivers, sit and stand, in the woods or on a crowded city street. In a broader sense, they have to know how to feel in the midst of a war, at a royal ball or wedding, in a department store. If you have time, it is also fun to do the same scenes in different historical settings. This involves research, but when reading classical plays it always helps to study the political, cultural, and social climate in which the plays were created and performed.

5. Pauses and silences are very important parts of the actor's repertoire.

If you are going to say something painful or momentous, a brief pause in the movement and a silence on stage prepares the audience for something to happen. Running sorrow into casual talk, or saying everything in the same tone and at the same speed kills the mystery of a performance. Yet novice actors are often so nervous that they do that without even knowing they are doing it. This is especially the case if one begins by having students memorize lines before doing spoken improvisations and by reading short classical speeches with attention to pauses and content.

I mentioned a number of voice improvisations in chapter 1. Another way to approach the development of a stage voice is to have students read short classical passages and experiment with different ways of saying the same lines. For example, a line as simple and famous as Hamlet's "To be or not to be, that is the question" has been delivered in hundreds of different ways by thousands of actors and can be used as a beginning exercise. First set the scene. Hamlet has to decide whether to kill himself because of all the demands made on him. One doesn't have to go much further than that to begin taking turns speaking the line. It can be said with passion, with fear, with cowardice, with wry amusement, or with scorn. It can be said slowly or thrown away. And silences can be used in almost any combination between the words. For example, here are three possibilities (the slash mark symbolizes a pause):

- To be/ or/ not to be// that is the question.
- To be// or not to be/ that// is the question.
- To be or not to be/// that is// the question.

Here's another quote from Shakespeare that elicits variation in delivery. It's from *Macbeth*:

Life's but a walking shadow, a poor player
That struts and frets his hour upon the stage,
And then is heard no more.

The last line itself can be rendered with pathos, irony, sarcasm, or even humor. Phrases such as "walking shadow" and "poor player" can become themes for improvisation. These three lines can become a first memory exercise that is integrated with improvisation and interpretation. (A good source of other lines and phrases to use is *Bartlett's Familiar Quotations.*)

After playing with lines, it makes sense to read short scenes aloud with students and to add gesture and movement when students are ready. There are many paperback collections of scenes for student actors to draw upon. Good ones are:

• *The Actor's Scenebook* (Vols. 1 and 2) edited by Michael Schulman and Eva Mekler.

• *Great Scenes from the World Theater* (Vols. 1 and 2) edited by James L. Steffensen.

Chapter 3
Monologues and Dialogues: Some Thoughts on Helping Students Begin to Write Plays

Student-created plays develop through improvisation particularly well with young children.

Young children can also dictate plays, and these scripts can be used to teach reading, as well as for performance. Older students can write their own plays and read each other's work. My students love to give class readings of each other's plays and the playwrights find the readings helpful in revising their work for performance.

Writing and performing a play involves:

• creating characters and developing a story around them

• feeling that others might be interested in seeing that story performed

• having people who like the story enough to spend their time rehearsing and transforming it into a live performance they are proud of

• finding an audience and a place where the performance can convincingly present the play's illusion.

One of my approaches to playwriting with young people is the progressive development of *monologues, dialogues, and scenes.*

Monologues

A monologue is delivered by one person with no response from any other character. There are many different kinds of monologues in the theater, so it makes sense, before asking students to write their own monologues, for you to describe and give examples of a number of them. Below are some common types of monologue that young people can work with in an improvisational context or recite in class. The reading list of any English class is also a source for monologues. Monologues in novels, as well as autobiographies and collections of letters, work just as well as selections from plays.

Reading monologues in the voice of a character in a play is not easy for youngsters unaccustomed to doing theater. Therefore I read a number of monologues to my students before suggesting they read. First I try to set the character and describe the play a bit. Sometimes I read in a flat boring voice and suggest that someone read the same monologue with more emotion. At other times I overact, or else do a monologue in the best way I can. I like to vary the way monologues are introduced and have students try each monologue and render it in a slightly different way. Sometimes, if the monologue is short, everyone in the room will take a turn reading it. The goal is to develop control of one's voice and an ability to render a character that might not resemble you at all.

Below are examples of different forms of monologue. (If any of my examples are inappropriate for your students, you should be able to find others in children's books, collections of nursery rhymes, fairy tales, or in the genre of children's books that makes extensive use of personal diaries.)

1. Stepping out of the play, moving to the front of the stage and speaking in character directly to the audience.

Example: A monologue from Peter Shaffer's play *Amadeus*. Salieri, a composer deeply envious of Mozart's genius, speaks to the audience and informs them of the context of the play. Talk with your students about Salieri's frustration in the face of Mozart's genius, which made it possible for music to flow from him with apparent ease, whereas Salieri had to work just to be competent.

You can also use, as background music for the reading of this selection, some compositions written by the young Mozart. His "Twinkle, Twinkle Little Star" variation for piano is good for this.

Reading this monologue can lead to discussions of genius, envy, frustration, and music, and can help students create their own monologues on related themes.

SALIERI: Can you hear them? Vienna is a City of Slander. Everyone tells tales here: even my servants. I keep only two now—*[He indicates them]*—they've been with me ever since I came here, fifty years ago. The Keeper of the Razor: The Maker of the Cakes. One keeps me tidy, the other keeps me full. Tonight, I gave them instructions they never heard before. *[To them]* 'Leave me, both of you! Tonight I do not go to bed at all!'

[They react in surprise.]

'Return here tomorrow morning at six precisely—to shave, to feed your capricious master!' *[He smiles at them both and claps his hands in gentle dismissal.]* Via. Via, via, via! Grazie!

[They bow, bewildered, and leave the stage.]

How surprised they were!...They'll be even more surprised tomorrow: indeed they will! *[He peers hard at the audience, trying to see it.]* Oh, won't you appear? I need you — desperately! This is now the last hour of my life. Those about to die implore you! What must I do to make you visible? Raise you up in the flesh to be my last, last audience?...

Does it take an Invocation? That's how it's always done in opera! Ah yes, of course: that's it. An *Invocation!* The only way *[He rises.]* Let me try to conjure you *now*—Ghosts of the distant Future—so that I can see you.

[He gets out of the wheelchair and huddles over to the fortepiano. He stands at the instrument and begins to sing in a high cracked voice, interrupting himself at the end of each sentence with figurations on the keyboard in the manner of a recitativo secco. *During this the house lights slowly come up to illuminate the audience.]*

[Singing]

Ghosts of the Future!

Shades of Time to come!

So much more unavoidable than those of Time gone by!

Appear with what sympathy Incarnation may endow you!

Appear You—

The yet-to-be-born!

The yet-to-hate!

The yet-to-*kill!*

Appear — Posterity!

[The light on the audience reaches its maximum. It stays like this during all of the following.]

[Speaking again] There. It worked. I can see you! That is the result of proper training. I was taught invocation by Chevalier Gluck, who was a true master at it. He had to be. In his day that is what people went to

42

the opera for: the raising of Gods, and Ghosts...Nowadays, since Rossini became the rage, they prefer to watch the escapades of hairdressers.

For younger children, the first pages of Ursula LeGuin's *Very Far Away from Anywhere Else* can be read as a monologue and can lead to discussions of conformity, identity, and learning about your own uniqueness. Lots of interesting writing, including monologues, can come out of this.

If you'd like a story about how I won my basketball letter and achieved fame, love, and fortune, don't read this. I don't know what I achieved in the six months I'm going to tell about. I achieved something, all right, but I think it may take me the rest of my life to find out what.

I never won any letters for anything. When I was a little kid, I really liked touch football, the strategy of it, but being short for my age I was always a bit slow even though I was good at evasive tactics. And then when we got into high school, it all got so organized. Going out for teams and wearing uniforms and all that stuff. And people talk about it all the time. Sports are neat to do, but dull to talk about. Anyhow there won't be much about sports in this.

I am talking into a tape recorder and then typing it. I tried to just write it, but it came out all stuffy and clotted-up with words, so let's see how it goes this way. My name is Owen Thomas Griffiths. I was seventeen in November. I am still fairly short for my age—5'7". I guess I will be short for my age when I'm forty-five, so what's the difference? It bothered me a lot when I was twelve or thirteen, but I was much shorter then compared to other kids, a genuine shrimp. At fifteen I grew six inches in eight months and felt really awful while I was doing it; my knees used to feel like the Bamboo Splinter Torture, but when it was over I was such a giant compared to what I had been that I never could really regret not going on any higher. I am average compact build and have dirty gray eyes and a lot of hair. The hair is curly, and whether I wear it short or long it sticks out all over my head. I fight it with a hairbrush every morning, and lose. I like my hair. It has a lot of willpower. However, this story is not about my hair, either.

I am always the youngest person in my class. And the youngest person in my family, being the only child. They let me into school early because I was such a bright little jerk. I have always been bright for my age. Who knows, at forty-five I may still be bright for my age. That is partly what this thing I'm telling, this story, is about. About being a bright little jerk.

43

It's OK, you know, up to about the sixth grade. Nobody really cares, least of all yourself. The teachers are mostly pretty nice to you, because you're easy to teach. Some of them love you for it, and give you neat books for extra reading. Some of them resent it, but they're too busy with the Behavior Problem types to have time to really make you feel lousy for being ahead of the others in math and reading. And there's always a few other kids, usually girls, who are as smart as you are, or smarter, and you and they write the class skits, and make lists for the teacher, and so on. And besides, for all the talk about how cruel little kids are, they haven't got a patch on older people for cruelty. Little kids are just dumb, the smart ones and the slow ones. They do dumb things. They say what they think. They haven't learned enough yet to say what they don't really think. That comes later, when kids begin to turn into people and find out that they are alone.

2. Stepping out of character and talking to the audience not as a character in the play, but as an actor or friend.

Example: From the play *Ododo* by Joseph A. Walker. In this selection, the actress (it could be an actor as well) addresses the audience as an actress and not as a character in a play.

He was long.
His fingers were long.
His arms were long.
He was long.
The muscles of his back were long.
From shoulder to shoulder he was long.
He was long.
His hair was black and bushy and long—
Like spruce trees on a hilltop.
He stretched all the way from the earth's center
To the top of Kilimanjaro
He stretched all the way from the valley
To the noonday sun.
He could work long.
He could play long.
He could laugh long.
He had cried so long inside
Until his tears had too long to go
To reach the outside.
It was a long time before he knew how
Long he was.

But they knew,
And they envied him long,
And they desired him long,
And all because a dark brown color
Covered his whole length
And painted the whole length of his long, long soul.

3. Making an aside either to the audience or to oneself during the course of the play as the rest of the action freezes.

Example: In William Saroyan's *The Time of Your Life*, Kitty talks of her dreams and desires. Joe's line at the beginning of the monologue can be delivered by Kitty or another character, or simply eliminated.

JOE: What's the dream now, Kitty Duval?
KITTY: *(dreaming the words and pictures.)* I dream of home. Christ, I always dream of home. I've no *home*. I've no place. But I always dream of all of us together again. We had a farm in Ohio. There was nothing good about it. It was always sad. There was always trouble. But I always dream about it as if I could go back and Papa would be there and Mamma and Louie and my little brother Stephen and my sister Mary. I'm Polish. Duval! My name isn't Duval, it's Koranovsky. Katerina Koranovsky. We lost everything. The house, the farm, the trees, the horses, the cows, the chickens. Papa died. He was old. He was thirteen years older than Mamma. We moved to Chicago. We tried to work. We tried to stay together. Louie got into trouble. The fellows he was with killed him for something. I don't know what. Stephen ran away from home. Seventeen years old. I don't know where he is. Then Mamma died. *(pause)* What's the dream? I dream of home.

4. Letting the audience in on things the characters don't know.

Example: The Stage Manager in Thornton Wilder's *Our Town* walks out onto an empty stage, places some tables and chairs, and begins telling the audience, in his omniscient way, all about Grover's Corners, New Hampshire, "our town." (Virtually every school library has a copy of this play.)

5. Addressing a character who has just left the stage, or addressing oneself.

Example: Puck, in Shakespeare's *A Midsummer Night's Dream*, tries to reassure himself that he has found the right person to enchant.

PUCK: Through the forest have I gone.
But Athenian found I none,
On whose eyes I might approve
This flower's force in stirring love.
Night and silence—Who is there?
Weeds of Athens he doth wear:
This is he, my master said,
Despised the Athenian maid;
And here the maiden, sleeping sound,
On the dank and dirty ground.
Pretty soul! She durst not lie
Near this lack-love, this kill-courtesy.
Churl, upon thy eyes I throw
All the power this charm doth owe.
When thou wakest, let love forbid
Sleep his seat on thy eyelid:
So awake when I am gone;
For I must now to Oberon.

6. Being on stage alone and speaking in character about something on your mind that is relevant to the action of the play.

Example: Linda, Willie Loman's wife in Arthur Miller's *Death of a Salesman*, is at Willie's grave and is speaking her last words to him.

LINDA: I'll be with you in a minute. Go on, Charley. I want to, just for a minute. I never had a chance to say good-by. *(Linda sits there, summoning herself.)* Forgive me, dear. I can't cry. I don't know what it is, but I can't cry. I don't understand it. Why did you ever do that? Help me, Willy, I can't cry. It seems to me that you're just on another trip. I keep expecting you. Willy, dear, I can't cry. Why did you do it? I search and search and I search, and I can't understand it, Willy. I made the last payment on the house today. Today, dear. And there'll be nobody home. *(A sob rises in her throat)* We're free and clear. *(Sobbing more fully, released)* We're free. *(Biff comes slowly toward her)* We're free...We're free... *(Linda sobs quietly [and turns to walk off right to her sons.])*

7. Speaking to a character who is not seen and may not be real.

Example for younger children: Briony, a young girl, is addressing a falcon that is chained to its perch.

A falcon is crouched on its perch, a chain round his leg. BRIONY is stroking his feathers, looking nervously round her.

BRIONY: Poor falcon, poor bird. . .how you long to fly away. This cave frightens you, my dear, and oh, how it frightens me! I have often heard talk of the Sorcerer's hunting-lodge, halfway up to the castle on the top of the mountain. Here he brings his poor captives from the forest, and when he has taken them from this place to the castle. . .there, who can tell what happens to them? Restless bird, you are throbbing with fear. How you hate the chain on your leg. I would loose you if I could. . .but I am a prisoner, too. Those bars hold me, as helpless as you. Don't look at me, falcon. . .turn your eyes away. . .I can do nothing.

(She goes to the barred archway, and looks out into the dark.)

The doorway into the forest is barred, and fastened with spells. And will not open until the Sorcerer returns.

(She runs back to the fireplace, and covers her face.)

What will he do with me? Surely he'll not harm me, for my mother holds his son. . .oh, but he knows she will never hurt Bat. Who is coming. . . there's someone coming. . .oh, not yet! Not yet!

—from *The Hunters and the Henwife* by Nicholas Stuart Gray

Another example: Elwood is the only one who sees Harvey, an imaginary rabbit. There are two moments below. In one, Elwood describes his first meeting with Harvey. This can be done as a dialogue or turned into a monologue. The second selection requires only Elwood (and his invisible and silent rabbit). The play is *Harvey* by Mary Chase.

ELWOOD: *(Sits, as KELLY sits R. of desk.)* Harvey and I sit in the bars and we have a drink or two and play the jukebox. Soon the faces of the other people turn toward mine and smile. They are saying: "We don't know your name, Mister, but you're a lovely fellow." Harvey and I warm ourselves in all these golden moments. We have entered as strangers— soon we have friends. They come over. They sit with us. They drink with us. They talk to us. They tell about the big terrible things they have done. The big wonderful things they *will* do. Their hopes, their regrets, their loves, their hates. All very large because nobody ever brings anything small into a bar. Then I introduce them to Harvey. And he is bigger and grander than anything they offer me. When they leave, they leave impressed. The same people seldom come back—but that's envy, my dear. There's a little bit of envy in the best of us—too bad, isn't it?

SANDERSON: *(Leaning forward.)* How did you happen to call him Harvey?

ELWOOD: Harvey is his name.

SANDERSON: How do you know that?

ELWOOD: That was rather an interesting coincidence, Doctor. One night several years ago I was walking early in the evening along Fairfax Street—between 18th and 19th. You know that block?

SANDERSON: Yes, yes.

ELWOOD: I had just helped Ed Hickey into a taxi. Ed had been mixing his rye with his gin, and I felt he needed conveying. I started to walk down the street when I heard a voice saying: "Good evening, Mr. Dowd." I turned and there was this great white rabbit leaning against a lamp-post. Well, I thought nothing of that, because when you have lived in a town as long as I have lived in this one, you get used to the fact that everybody knows your name. Naturally, I went over to chat with him. He said to me: "Ed Hickey is a little spiffed this evening, or could I be mistaken?" Well, of course he was not mistaken. I think the world and all of Ed but he was spiffed. Well, anyway, we stood there and talked, and finally I said—"You have the advantage of me. You know my name and I don't know yours." Right back at me he said: "What name do you like?" Well, I didn't even have to think a minute: Harvey has always been my favorite name. So I said, "Harvey," and this is the interesting part of the whole thing. He said—"What a coincidence! My name happens to be Harvey."

•

ELWOOD: Aunt Ethel—I want you to meet Harvey. As you can see he's a Pooka. *(Turns toward air beside him.)* Harvey, you've heard me speak of Mrs. Chauvenet? We always called her Aunt Ethel. She is one of my oldest and dearest friends. *(Inclines head toward space and goes "Hmmm!" and then listens as though not hearing first time. Nods as though having heard someone next to him speak.)* Yes — yes — that's right. She's the one. This is the one. *(To MRS. CHAUVENET.)* He says he would have known you anywhere. *(Then as a confused, bewildered look comes over MRS. CHAUVENET's face and as she looks to L. and R. of ELWOOD and cranes her neck to see behind him—ELWOOD not seeing her expression, crosses her towards VETA and MYRTLE MAE)* You both look lovely. *(Turns to the air next to him.)* Come on in with me, Harvey—We must say hello to all of our friends—(Bows to MRS. CHAUVENET.)* I beg your pardon, Aunt Ethel. If you'll excuse me for one moment— *(Puts his hand gently on her arm, trying to turn her.)*

MRS. CHAUVENET: What?

ELWOOD: You are standing in his way—*(She gives a little—her eyes wide on him.)* Come along, Harvey. *(He watches the invisible Harvey cross to door, then stops him.)* Uh-uh! *(ELWOOD goes over to door. He turns and pantomimes as he arranges the tie and brushes off the head of the invisible Harvey. Then he does the same thing to his own tie. They are all watching him, MRS. CHAUVENET in horrified fascination. The heads of VETA and MYRTLE, bowed in agony.)* Go right on in, Harvey. I'll join you in a minute. *(He pantomimes as though slapping him on the back, and ushers him out. Then turns and comes back to MRS. CHAUVENET.)* Aunt Ethel, I can see you are disturbed about Harvey. Please don't be. He stares like that at everybody. It's his way. But he liked you. I could tell. He liked you very much. *(Pats her arm reassuringly, smiles at her, then calmly and confidently goes on out at R.)*

8. A self-contained monologue that forms a miniplay, complete in itself.

Example: Toshio Mori's *The Woman Who Makes Swell Doughnuts*, in effect a lovely self-contained playlet that provides much insight into Japanese-American culture.

There is nothing I like to do better than to go to her house and knock on the door and when she opens the door, to go in. It is one of the experiences I will long remember—perhaps the only immortality that I will ever be lucky to meet in my short life—and when I say experience I do not mean the actual movement, the motor of our lives. I mean by experience the dancing of emotions before our eyes and inside of us, the dance that is still but is the roar and the force capable of stirring the earth and the people.

Of course, she, the woman I visit, is old and of her youthful beauty there is little left. Her face of today is coarse with hard water and there is no question that she has lived her life: given birth to six children, worked side by side with her man for forty years, working in the fields, working in the house, caring for the grandchildren, facing the summers and winters and also the springs and autumns, running the household that is completely her little world. And when I came on the scene, when I discovered her in her little house on Seventh Street, all of her life was behind, all of her task in this world was tabbed, looked into, thoroughly attended, and all that is before her in life and the world, all that could be before her now was to sit and be served; duty done, work done, time clock punched; old-age pension or old-age security; easy chair; soft serene hours till death take her. But this was not of her, not the least bit of her.

49

When I visit her she takes me to the coziest chair in the living room, where are her magazines and books in Japanese and English. "Sit down," she says. "Make yourself comfortable. I will come back with some hot doughnuts just out of oil."

And before I can turn a page of a magazine she is back with a plateful of hot doughnuts. There is nothing I can do to describe her doughnut; it is in a class by itself, without words, without demonstration. It is a doughnut, just a plain doughnut just out of oil but it is different, unique. Perhaps when I am eating her doughnuts I am really eating her; I have this foolish notion in my head many times and whenever I catch myself doing so I say, that is not so, that is not true. Her doughnuts really taste swell, she is the best cook I have ever known, Oriental dishes or American dishes.

I bow humbly that such a room, such a house exists in my neighborhood so I may dash in and out when my spirit wanes, when hell is loose. I sing gratefully that such a simple and common experience becomes an event that is a part of me, an addition to the elements of the earth, water, fire, and air, and I seek the day when it will become a part of everyone.

All her friends, old and young, call her Mama. Everybody calls her Mama. That is not new, it is logical. I suppose there is in every block of every city in America a woman who can be called Mama by her friends and the strangers meeting her. This is commonplace, it is not new and the old sentimentality may be the undoing of the moniker. But what of a woman who isn't a mama but is, and instead of priding in the expansion of her little world, takes her little circle, living out her days in the little circle, perhaps never to be exploited in a biography or on everybody's tongue, but enclosed, shut, excluded from world news and newsreels; just sitting, just moving, just alive, planting the plants in the fields, caring for the children and the grandchildren and baking the tastiest doughnuts this side of the next world.

When I sit with her I do not need to ask deep questions, I do not need to know Plato or The Sacred Books of the East or dancing. I do not need to be on guard. But I am on guard and foot-loose because the room is alive.

"Where are the grandchildren?" I say. "Where are Mickey, Tadao, and Yaeko?"

"They are out in the yard," she says. "I say to them, play, play hard, go out there and play hard. You will be glad later for everything you have done with all your might."

Sometimes we sit many minutes in silence. Silence does not bother her. She says silence is the most beautiful symphony, she says the air breathed in silence is sweeter and sadder. That is about all we talk of. Sometimes I sit and gaze out the window and watch the Southern Pacific trains rumble by and the vehicles whiz with speed. And sometimes she catches me doing this and she nods her head and I know she understands that I think the silence in the room is great, and also the roar and the dust of the outside is great, and when she is nodding I understand that she is saying that this, her little room, her little circle, is a depot, a pause, for the weary traveler, but outside, outside of her little world there is dissonance, hugeness of another kind, and the travel to do. So she has her little house, she bakes the grandest doughnuts, and inside of her she houses a little depot.

Most stories would end with her death, would wait till she is peacefully dead and peacefully at rest but I cannot wait that long. I think she will grow, and her hot doughnuts just out of the oil will grow with softness and touch. And I think it would be a shame to talk of her doughnuts after she is dead, after she is formless.

Instead I take today to talk of her and her wonderful doughnuts when the earth is something to her, when the people from all parts of the earth may drop in and taste the flavor, her flavor, which is everyone's and all flavor; talk to her, sit with her, and also taste the silence of her room and the silence that is herself; and finally go away to hope and keep alive what is alive in her, on earth and in men, expressly myself.

9. A description of an event happening offstage.

Example: The following selection from Dylan Thomas' *Under Milk Wood* describes the setting.

FIRST VOICE *(Very Softly)* To begin at the beginning:
It is spring, moonless night in the small town, starless and bible-black, the cobblestreets silent and the hunched, courters'-and-rabbits' wood limping invisible down to the sloeblack, slow, black, crowblack, fishingboat-bobbing sea. The houses are blind as moles (though moles see fine to-night in the snouting, velvet dingles) or blind as Captain Cat there in the muffled middle by the pump and the town clock, the shops in mourning, the Welfare Hall in widows' weeds. And all the people of the lulled and dumbfound town are sleeping now.

Hush, the babies are sleeping, the farmers, the fishers, the tradesmen and pensioners, cobbler, schoolteacher, postman and publican, the undertaker and fancy woman, drunkard, dressmaker, preacher, policeman, the webfoot cocklewoman and the tidy wives. Young girls lie bedded soft or glide in their dreams, with rings and trousseaux, bridesmaided by glowworms down the aisles of the organplaying wood. The boys are dreaming wicked of the bucking ranches of the night and the jolly-rodgered sea. And the anthracite statues of the horses sleep in the fields, and the cows in the byres, and the dogs in the wet-nosed yards; and the cats nap in the slant corners or lope sly, streaking and needling, on the one cloud of the roofs.

You can hear the dew falling, and the hushed town breathing. Only *your* eyes are unclosed to see the black and folded town fast, and slow, asleep. And you alone can hear the invisible starfall, the darkest-before-dawn minutely dewgrazed stir of the black, dab-filled sea where the *Arethusa,* the *Curlew* and the *Skylark, Zanzibar, Rhiannon,* the *Rover*, the *Cormorant,* and the *Star of Wales* tilt and ride.

Listen. It is night moving in the streets, the processional salt slow musical wind in Coronation Street and Cockle Row, it is the grass growing on the Llaregyb Hill, dewfall, starfall, the sleep of birds in Milk Wood.

10. Waiting for someone.

Example: This monologue (from Samuel Beckett's *Waiting for Godot*) is one of many dealing with the unfulfilled expectations in the play.

VLADIMIR: Let us not waste our time in idle discourse! *(Pause, Vehemently.)* Let us do something, while we have the chance! It is not every day that we are needed. Not indeed that we personally are needed. Others would meet the case equally well, if not better. To all mankind they were addressed, those cries for help still ringing in our ears! But at this place, at this moment of time, all mankind is us, whether we like it or not. Let us make the most of it, before it is too late! Let us represent worthily for once the foul brood to which a cruel fate consigned us! What do you say? *(Estragon says nothing.)* It is true that when with folded arms we weigh the pros and cons we are no less a credit to our species. The tiger bounds to the help of his congeners without the least reflexion, or else he slinks away into the depths of the thickets. But that is not the question. What are we doing here, *that* is the question. And we are blessed in this, that we happen to know the answer. Yes, in this immense confusion one thing alone is clear. We are waiting for Godot to come—

11. A telephone call.

Example: *A Woman Alone* by Dario Fo and Frana Rame is a one-woman play about sexism, fear, and revolt.

Lights up on a woman downstage center, ironing. She's in her early thirties dressed in a more or less see-through negligee and high heeled slippers. A portable radio is playing pop music very loud. There are   ART:

52

five doors leading off. She plays throughout as if facing a window which is only a few feet away from the window of the flat opposite. Bored and expressionless, she irons in rhythm to the music, executing sketchy dance steps. At one point she raises her arms and, with the iron in one hand, moves her arms to the music. Suddenly her face lights up with surprise and pleasure. She comes further downstage.

Hey! Hey Signora, good morning! *(Louder)* I said good morning! How long have you been living over there? *(Shouts)* I said how long ago did you move in? I thought that apartment was still empty. I'm so glad somebody's moved in. What? *(Even louder)* I said I'm glad! I'm glad! What's the matter, can't you hear me? What? The what? Oh yes. Right. Wait.

She runs over to the radio and turns it off and goes back to window.

Sorry. When I'm on my own I always have the radio on. If it isn't turned up full blast I get this feeling I might hang myself. I've got the stereo on in the living room. Listen.

Goes to living room door and opens it. Blast of classical music. The music cuts off as she shuts the door.

Did you hear it? And the cassette player's going in the kitchen.

Goes to kitchen door, opens it, blast of jazz, closes it.

See? Whatever room I go into I've got company. What? *(Shocked)* Oh not the bedroom, of course no! My goodness no. I've got the television on in there.

Goes to bedroom door. Opens it. Blast of plain chant.

(Shouts) Oh yes I always keep it pretty loud. That's a high mass! In Polish *(Music cuts off as she shuts the door)* Polish. . .what a daft language, eh? You can't understand a word of it. Just right for a pope!

She goes back to her ironing.

Oh yes I like Church music too even though it's really hopeless to dance to. Any kind of music really, as long as it's loud. It keeps me company, you see. How do you keep yourself company, Signora? Ahhh . . .a child! Aren't you lucky!

Pause. Looks at the small jacket she's been pressing.

How silly I am. I've got a child myself. Two! A big one and a little one.

Brings the jacket further downstage, sits and brushes it.

No no, they don't keep me company, oh no. The big one's started school and she's got her own friends. The little boy's at home the whole time but he's no company either. He's too young. He's a baby. . .even though he snores like an old man. Sleep? Sleeps all the time! *(Sighs)* If only he'd grow up. *(Then hastily bright)* But I'm not complaining. I love it at home. I've got everything. My husband gives me everything I need. Like. . . like I've got. . . .*(Looks round). . .*I've got a refrigerator! What?

Well yes I know everybody has refrigerators but mine *(Impressive)* makes round ice cubes. *(Serious again)* And I've got a washing machine with twenty four different programs. There's one that's for such delicate things I could wash paper in it...I could! Trouble is I never have any paper to wash. And a dryer too. You would not believe how dry this dryer dries. Amazing. Sometimes I have to get all the clothes wet again...they're too dry to iron.

12. A metaphysical plea or prayer, a hallucination, or a prophesy.

Example: Macbeth, who is driven to commit murder, sees a vision of a dagger before him and broods about murder before he draws his "palpable" dagger.

> MACBETH: Go bid thy mistress, when my drink is ready,
> She strike upon the bell. Get thee to bed.
> *(Exit Servant.)*
> Is this a dagger which I see before me,
> The handle toward my hand? Come, let me clutch thee.
> I have thee not, and yet I see thee still.
> Art thou not, fatal vision, sensible
> To feeling as to sight? or art thou but
> A dagger of the mind, a false creation,
> Proceeding from the heat-oppressed brain?
> I see thee yet, in form as palpable
> As this which now I draw.
> Thou marshal'st me the way that I was going;
> And such an instrument I was to use.
> Mine eyes are made the fools o' the other senses,
> Or else worth all the rest: I see thee still.
> And on thy blade and dudgeon gouts of blood,
> Which was not so before.
> There's no such thing:
> It is the bloody business which informs
> Thus to mine eyes. Now o'er the one half-world
> Nature seems dead, and wicked dreams abuse
> The curtain'd sleep; witchcraft celebrates
> Pale Hecate's offerings; and wither'd murder,
> Alarum'd by his sentinel, the wolf,
> Whose howl's his watch, thus with his stealthy pace,
> With Tarquin's ravishing strides, towards his design

Moves like a ghost. Thou sure and firm-set earth,
Hear not my steps, which way they walk, for fear
Thy very stones prate of my whereabout,
And take the present horror from the time,
Which now suits with it. Whiles I threat, he lives:
Words to the heat of deeds too cold breath gives.
(A bell rings.)
I go, and it is done: the bell invites me.
Hear it not, Duncan, for it is a knell
That summons thee to heaven, or to hell.

13. An excerpt spoken by one of the characters, with no response from the other characters.

Example for younger children: This excerpt from James Reeves' *The King Who Took Sunshine* involves the use of sound effects and props. After reading the monologue aloud, it's fun to improvise the sounds of water and wind, as well as have children put on cotton beards and then do the monologue with sound effects, props, and gestures.

Joanna is the daughter of the King and Queen of Portamento. This country is badly in need of money and the King wants her to marry a wealthy Duke; but Joanna is secretly in love with Godolphin, the kitchen-boy.

JOANNA: *(Enters carrying a pair of slippers)* Good-evening, Father. *(Kissing him)* Have you had a very tiring day? Here, sit down and let me put them on. . . That's right. Oh, I'll be careful of your chilblains. Is that more comfortable? Father, I have been thinking about a suitable husband, but I have come to the conclusion that I'm much too young to marry; in fact I don't mean to get married for years and years. What's that? The Duke of Monte Rosa? That sounds nice. What's he like? How old is he? When can I see him? *(The King hands her the portrait, which Joanna and the Queen examine in silent amazement)* You can't mean it. Not that old scarecrow? Father, I. . .I. . .His nose—it's all over the place. His eyes—they don't both look the same way. Father, I don't want to be married at all, and if I did, that odious old circus-freak would be the last man on earth I should choose. I won't marry him—I won't, I won't, I won't. *(She stamps her feet furiously)* Mother, I don't have to marry that man, do I? Oh, do say something, Mother! surely you can't want to marry your only daughter to *that!* I won't have him, I tell you, I won't.

(The King storms out. Joanna throws herself on the settee and sobs angrily. The Queen tries to comfort her.)

He has no right to marry me to a man I can't stand the sight of. Do go and stop him! Tell him I'll run away! Tell him I'll kill myself! I never will marry that trampled-on sponge-cake, that suet pudding with whiskers, that—oh, it's too bad, it's terrible. Leave me alone, Mother. Go and tell him what I've said.

Another example for fifth-grade to junior high students, from Carson McCullers' *The Member of the Wedding*:

Frankie, who is speaking, is twelve years old. Her brother is about to get married and she fantasizes that she will stay with her brother and his wife and do all of the things they will do. She hopes to be a member of the marriage as well as a member of the wedding.

FRANKIE: Boyoman! Manoboy! When we leave Winter Hill we're going to more places than you ever thought about or even knew existed. Just where we'll go first I don't know and it don't matter. Because after we go to that place we're going on to another. Alaska, China, Iceland, South America! Travelling on trains! Letting her rip on motor cycles! Flying around all over the world in aeroplanes! Here today and gone tomorrow! All over the world. It's the damn truth! Boyoman! . . . And talking of things happening, things will happen so fast we won't hardly have time to realize them. Captain Jarvis Addams wins highest medals and is decorated by the President. Miss F. Jasmine Addams beats all records. Mrs. Janice Addams selected Miss United Nations in a Beauty Contest. One thing after another happening so fast we don't hardly notice them. . . . And we will meet everybody. We will just walk up to people and know them right away. We will be walking down a dark road and see a lighted house and knock on the door and strangers will rush to meet us and say, "Come in! Come in!" We will know decorated aviators and New York people and movie stars. We will have thousands and thousands of friends. And we will belong to so many clubs that we can't even keep track of all of them. We will be members of the whole world. Boyoman! Manoboy!

Example for older students: This speech from Shakespeare's *Julius Caesar* is delivered at Caesar's funeral before hundreds of people. Marc Antony's address, however, is to the dead Caesar as well as to the crowd, and could be seen as a monologue.

ANTONY: Friends, Romans, countrymen, lend me your ears;
I come to bury Caesar, not to praise him.
The evil that men do lives after them;

The good is oft interred with their bones;
So let it be with Caesar. The noble Brutus
Hath told you Caesar was ambitious:
If it were so, it was a grievous fault,
And grievously hath Caesar answer'd it,
Here, under leave of Brutus and the rest, —
For Brutus is an honorable man;
So are they all, all honorable men, —
Come I to speak in Caesar's funeral.
He was my friend, faithful and just to me:
But Brutus says he was ambitious;
And Brutus is an honorable man.
He hath brought many captives home to Rome,
Whose ransoms did the general coffers fill:
Did this in Caesar seem ambitious?
When that the poor have cried, Caesar hath wept:
Ambition should be made of sterner stuff:
Yet Brutus says he was ambitious;
And Brutus is an honorable man.
You all did see that on the Lupercal
I thrice presented him a kingly crown,
Which he did thrice refuse: was this ambition?
Yet Brutus says he was ambitious;
And, sure, he is an honorable man.
I speak not to disprove what Brutus spoke,
But here I am to speak what I do know.
You all did love him once, not without cause:
What cause withholds you then to mourn for him?
O judgment! Thou art fled to brutish beasts,
And men have lost their reason. Bear with me;
My heart is in the coffin there with Caesar,
And I must pause till it come back to me.

14. A remembering, a reflection on the past spoken to oneself or the audience.

Example: In this excerpt from Maxwell Anderson's *Winterset*, Mio reflects upon her father who has been unjustly imprisoned and executed for advocating justice for the poor. Her father's character is derived from Sacco and Vanzetti, two anarchists who were executed in Boston in the early part of this century after a trial that, in retrospect, was unjust.

MIO: When I was four years old
we climbed through an iron gate, my mother and I,
to see my father in prison. He stood in the death-cell
and put his hand through the bars and said, My Mio,
I have only this to leave you, that I love you
and will love you after I die. Love me then, Mio,
when this hard thing comes on you, that you must live
a man despised for your father. That night the guards,
walking in flood-lights brighter than high noon,
led him between them with his trousers slit
and a shaven head for the cathodes. This sleet and rain
that I feel cold here on my face and hands
will find him under thirteen years of clay
in prison ground. Lie still and rest, my father,
for I have not forgotten. When I forget
may I lie blind as you. No other love,
time passing, nor the spaced light-years of suns
shall blur your voice, or tempt me from the path
that clears your name—
till I have these rats in my grip
or sleep deep where you sleep.

The examples I have chosen are most appropriate for older students, but the modes they represent and the themes they embody can be found in literature for younger people. For example, it is possible to pull a passage from a book in which one character is addressing another and turn it into a monologue. Here's such a passage, from Astrid Lindgren's *Pippi Longstocking*:

The teacher decided to give up arithmetic altogether. She thought maybe Pippi would prefer to learn to read. So she took out a pretty little card with a picture of an ibex on it. In front of the ibex's nose was the letter "i."

"Now, Pippi," she said briskly, "you'll see something jolly. You see here an ibex. And the letter in front of this ibex is called *i*."

"That I'll never believe," said Pippi. "I think it looks exactly like a straight line with a little fly speck over it. But what I'd really like to know is, what has the ibex to do with the fly speck?"

The teacher took out another card with a picture of a snake on it and told Pippi that the letter on that was an *s*.

"Speaking of snakes," said Pippi, "I'll never, ever forget the time I had a fight with a huge snake in India. You can't imagine what a dreadful snake it was, fourteen yards long and mad as a hornet, and every day he ate up five Indians and then two little children for dessert, and one time he came and wanted me for dessert, and he wound himself around me—uhhh!—but I've been around a bit, I said, and hit him in the head, bang, and then he hissed uiuiuiuiuiuiuitch, and then I hit him again, and bingo! he was dead, and, indeed, so that is the letter *s*—most remarkable!"

Pippi had to stop to get her breath. And the teacher, who had now begun to think that Pippi was an unruly and troublesome child, decided that the class should have drawing for a while.

Pippi's story can be excerpted and turned into a simple monologue by using only the paragraph that begins, "Speaking of snakes. . . ."

One way to introduce this monologue is to read all or part of the book to the class, and then talk about how Pippi might speak. Then students can take turns speaking as Pippi.

Another way would be to begin with the monologue and, before introducing students to Pippi, have them figure out who might be telling the story.

Here are two selections from fictional diaries that make good monologues. One way to read these is have students sit at a desk in front of the class and pretend to be writing the diaries as they speak them.

The first diary is from Sue Townsend's *The Growing Pains of Adrian Mole*. Adrian is about fourteen at the time. The British are about to engage in a war with Argentina in the Falkland Islands. It makes sense to locate the Falklands, Argentina, and Great Britain on a map before reading this hilarious and somewhat bittersweet selection.

Sunday   April 4th
My father has sent a telegram to the War Office. He wants to take part in the war with Argentina. His telegram read:
QUALIFIED HEATING ENGINEER STOP A1 FITNESS STOP OFFERS HIMSELF IN THE SERVICE OF HIS COUNTRY STOP READY FOR IMMEDIATE MOBILIZATION

My mother says that my father will do anything to avoid working for Manpower Services as a canal bank renovator.

At tea-time I was looking at our world map, but I couldn't see the Falkland Islands anywhere. My mother found them; they were hidden under a crumb of fruitcake.

I feel guilty about mentioning a personal anguish at this time of national crisis, but ever since last night when a model aeroplane became stuck fast to my nose with glue, I have suffered torment. My nose has swollen up so much that I am frantic with worry that it might burst and take my brain with it.

I rang the Casualty Department and, after a lot of laughing, the nurse who removed the plane came on the line. She said that I was 'probably allergic to the glue', and that the swelling would go down in a few days. She added, 'Perhaps it will teach you not to sniff glue again.' I tried to explain but she put the phone down.

Pandora has been round but I declined to see her. She would go straight off me if she saw my repulsive nose.

Monday   April 5th
Just my luck! It is the first day of the school holidays and I can't go out because of my gigantic swollen nose. Even my mother is a bit worried about it now. She wanted to prick it with a sterilized needle, but I wouldn't let her. She can't sew an accurate patch on a pair of jeans with a needle, let alone do delicate medical procedures with one. I've begged her to take me to a private nose specialist, but she has refused. She says she needs the money for her 'Well Woman' test. She is having her primary and secondary sexual organs checked. Yuk!

The dog is in love with a cocker spaniel called Mitzi. The dog stands no chance, though: (a) it isn't a pedigree, and (b) it doesn't keep itself looking smart like most dogs. I tried to explain these things to the dog, but it just looked sad and mournful and went back to lying outside Mitzi's gate. Being in love is no joke. I have the same problem with Pandora that the dog has with Mitzi. We are both in a lower social class than our loved ones.

Tuesday   April 6th
The nation has been told that Britain and Argentina are not at war, we are at conflict.

I am reading *Scoop* by a woman called Evelyn Waugh.

Wednesday   April 7th
Wrote and sent Pandora a love letter and a poem. The letter said:
Pandora my love,

Due to an unfortunate physical disability I am unable to see you in person, but every fibre of my being cries out for your immediate physical proximity. Be patient, my love, soon we will laugh again.

Yours with undying love,

Adrian

PS. What are your views on the Argentinian conflict, with particular reference to Lord Carrington's resignation?

The Discontented Tuna
I am a Tuna fish,
Swimming in the sea of discontent.
Oh, when, when,
Will I find the spawning ground?

I hope Pandora sees through my poem and realizes the symbolism of 'spawning ground'. I am sick of being the only virgin in our class. Everybody but me is sexually experienced. Barry Kent boasts about how many housewives he makes love to on his father's milkround. He says they are the reason why he is always late for school.

The second diary is the central part of Guy de Maupassant's short story *The Diary of a Madman*. There is a short introduction and a short conclusion that can be read by one student (or the teacher) and another student can perform the diary as a monologue. The diary is found among the papers of an eighty-two-year-old judge who has just died. It is about his feelings about spending a life condemning people to death or prison.

He was dead — the head of a high tribunal, the upright magistrate, whose irreproachable life was a proverb in all the courts of France. Advocates, young counselors, judges, had saluted, bowing low in token of profound respect, remembering that grand face, pale and thin, illumined by two bright, deep-set eyes.

He had passed his life in pursuing crime and in protecting the weak. Swindlers and murderers had no more redoubtable enemy, for he seemed to read in the recesses of their souls their most secret thoughts.

He was dead, now, at the age of eighty-two, honored by the homage and followed by the regrets of a whole people. Soldiers in red breeches had escorted him to the tomb, and men in white cravats had shed on his grave tears that seemed to be real.

But listen to the strange paper found by the dismayed notary in the desk where the judge had kept filed the records of great criminals! It was entitled:

WHY?

June 20, 1851. I have just left court. I have condemned Blondel to death! Now, why did this man kill his five children? Frequently one meets with people to whom killing is a pleasure. Yes, yes, it should be a pleasure—the greatest of all, perhaps, for is not killing most like creating? To make and to destroy! These two words contain the history of the universe, the history of all worlds, all that is, all! Why is it not intoxicating to kill?

June 25. To think that there is a being who lives, who walks, who runs. A being? What is a being? An animated thing which bears in it the principle of motion, and a will ruling that principle. It clings to nothing, this thing, its feet are independent of the ground. It is a grain of life that moves on the earth, and this grain of life, coming I know not whence, one can destroy at one's will. Then nothing—nothing more. It perishes; it is finished.

June 26. Why, then, is it a crime to kill? Yes, why? On the contrary, it is the law of nature. Every being has the mission to kill; he kills to live, and he lives to kill. The beast kills without ceasing, all day, every instant of its existence. Man kills without ceasing, to nourish himself; but since in addition he needs to kill for pleasure, he has invented the chase! The child kills the insects he finds, the little birds, all the little animals that come in his way. But this does not suffice for the irresistible need of massacre that is in us. It is not enough to kill beasts; we must kill man too. Long ago this need was satisfied by human sacrifice. Now, the necessity of living in society has made murder a crime. We condemn and punish the assassin! But as we cannot live without yielding to this natural and imperious instinct of death, we relieve ourselves, from time to time, by wars. Then a whole nation slaughters another nation. It is a feast of blood, a feast that maddens armies and intoxicates the civilians, women, and children, who read, by lamplight at night, the feverish story of massacre.

And do we despise those picked out to accomplish these butcheries of men? No, they are loaded with honors. They are clad in gold and in resplendent stuffs; they wear plumes on their heads and ornaments on their breasts; and they are given crosses, rewards, titles of every kind. They are proud, respected, loved by women, cheered by the crowd, solely because their mission is to shed human blood! They drag through the streets their instruments of death, and the passer-by, clad in black, looks on with envy. For to kill is the great law put by nature in the heart of existence! There is nothing more beautiful and honorable than killing!

June 30. To kill is the law, because Nature loves eternal youth. She seems to cry in all her unconscious acts: "Quick! quick! quick!" The more she destroys, the more she renews herself.

July 3. It must be a pleasure, unique and full of zest, to kill: to place before you a living, thinking being; to make therein a little hole, nothing but a little hole, and to see that red liquid flow which is the blood, which is the life; and then to have before you only a heap of limp flesh, cold, inert, void of thought!

August 5. I, who have passed my life in judging, condemning, killing by words pronounced, killing by the guillotine those who had killed by the knife, if I should do as all the assassins whom I have smitten have done, I, I—who would know it?

August 10. Who would ever know? Who would ever suspect me, especially if I should choose a being I had no interest in doing away with?

August 22. I could resist no longer. I have killed a little creature as an experiment, as a beginning. Jean, my servant, had a goldfinch in a cage hung in the office window. I sent him on an errand, and I took the little bird in my hand, in my hand where I felt its heart beat. It was warm. I went up to my room. From time to time I squeezed it tighter; its heart beat faster; it was atrocious and delicious. I was nearly choking it. But I could not see the blood.

Then I took scissors, short nail scissors, and I cut its throat in three strokes, quite gently. It opened its bill, it struggled to escape me, but I held it, oh! I held it—I even could have held a mad dog—and I saw the blood trickle.

And then I did as assassins do—real ones. I washed the scissors and washed my hands. I sprinkled water, and took the body, the corpse, to the garden to hide it. I buried it under a strawberry plant. It will never be found. Every day I can eat a strawberry from that plant. How one can enjoy life, when one knows how!

My servant cried; he thought his bird flown. How could he suspect me? Ah!

August 25. I must kill a man! I must!

August 30. It is done. But what a little thing! I had gone for a walk in the forest of Vernes. I was thinking of nothing, literally nothing. See! a child on the road, a little child eating a slice of bread and butter. He stops to see me pass and says, "Good day, Mr. President."

And the thought enters my head: "Shall I kill him?"

I answer: "You are alone, my boy?"

"Yes, sir."

"All alone in the woods?"

"Yes, sir."

The wish to kill him intoxicated me like wine. I approached him quite softly, persuaded that he was going to run away. And suddenly I seized him by the throat. He held my wrists in his little hands, and his body writhed like a feather on the fire. Then he moved no more. I threw the body in the ditch, then some weeds on top of it. I returned home and dined well. What a little thing it was! In the evening I was very gay, light, rejuvenated, and passed the evening at the Prefect's. They found me witty. But I have not seen blood! I am not tranquil.

August 31. The body has been discovered. They are hunting for the assassin. Ah!

September 1. Two tramps have been arrested. Proofs are lacking.

September 2. The parents have been to see me. They wept! Ah!

October 6. Nothing has been discovered. Some strolling vagabond must have done the deed. Ah! If I had seen the blood flow it seems to me I should be tranquil now!

October 10. Yet another. I was walking by the river, after breakfast. And I saw, under a willow, a fisherman asleep. It was noon. A spade, as if expressly put there for me, was standing in a potato field near by.

I took it. I returned; I raised it like a club, and with one blow of the edge I cleft the fisherman's head. Oh! He bled, this one!—rose-colored blood. It flowed into the water quite gently. And I went away with a grave step. If I had been seen! Ah! I should have made an excellent assassin.

October 25. The affair of the fisherman makes a great noise. His nephew, who fished with him, is charged with the murder.

October 26. The examining magistrate affirms that the nephew is guilty. Everybody in town believes it. Ah! ah!

October 27. The nephew defends himself badly. He had gone to the village to buy bread and cheese, he declares. He swears that his uncle had been killed in his absence! Who would believe him?

October 28. The nephew has all but confessed, so much have they made him lose his head! Ah! Justice!

November 15. There are overwhelming proofs against the nephew, who was his uncle's heir. I shall preside at the sessions.

January 25, 1852. To death! to death! to death. I have had him condemned to death! The advocate-general spoke like an angel! Ah! Yet another! I shall go to see him executed!

March 10. It is done. They guillotined him this morning. He died very well! very well! That gave me pleasure! How fine it is to see a man's head cut off!

Now, I shall wait, I can wait. It would take such a little thing to let myself be caught.

The manuscript contained more pages, but told of no new crime.

Alienist physicians to whom the awful story has been submitted declare that there are in the world many unknown madmen, as adroit and as terrible as this monstrous lunatic.

Moving from delivering monologues to writing them can be made smooth by discussing the themes of the examples you present and suggesting that students write variations of them.

Another way is to begin with characters. Have students develop imaginary beings and then set them in some situation where they have to speak. The characters and situations can be as varied as:

• A baby bird that has fallen out of the nest

• A dog that has a new master

• An alien who has landed in the middle of New York City in the middle of the rush hour

• A parent whose child has just run away from home

• A person who is lost in the woods, on the streets, or in outer space

• A person going out on his or her first date.

As students begin to write their own monologues, here are some questions that can be used to stimulate and focus their work:

• Who is the character? Make up a name. Imagine how she or he looks. What does the character like or dislike doing? Try to visualize the character in different places: at work, at home, with other people, etc.

• Where does the monologue begin? What does the stage look like? What time of day is it? Is the scene indoors or outdoors? What historical period is it?

• What has preceded the monologue? Where has the character come from and where is the character going?

• Whom is the character addressing? Someone offstage, himself or herself, the audience, a god, an object, or an animal?

Once these are clarified, it's time to develop the monologue. This can be done either by writing or by talking it out first and then writing it down. However, dramatic monologues are written to be spoken and the author should be encouraged to read the work in progress aloud.

I've found it useful to do the exercise myself and read it to my students to give them an idea of the sort of writing that might develop. Here's one monologue I wrote while doing a series of lessons on playwriting with high school students:

Monologue Example
1. WHO IS THE CHARACTER?
Jon Rogers, nineteen years old. He wants to be a writer but everyone tells him that he doesn't have the talent and that he should go get a well-paying job and settle down.
2. WHAT DOES THE STAGE LOOK LIKE? WHERE IS THE CHARACTER?
It is night. The stage shows a park with a single bench and a streetlamp. Jon is sitting on the bench, downcast.
3. WHAT IN THE PLAY PRECEDES THE MONOLOGUE?
Jon has just had an argument with his parents. They told him only fools wanted to be writers and that he had to come to his senses, live in the real world, get his mind straightened out. He walked out of the house.
4. THE MONOLOGUE
JON: *(sitting hunched over, his hands clasped in front of him. His voice starts low and begins to get louder and louder.)* It's time to grow up, grow up grow up....that's all they say...grow up...to what, to a quiet house in a quiet street in a quiet town...to a soft job in a soft business in a not so soft world...to...I can just see it *(He gets up slowly.)* Jon Rogers, distinguished businessman, gets up early in the morning ...Jon Rogers, good citizen, comes home early at night...Jon Rogers, decent parent, sends his children to expensive camps and buys them computers...Jon Rogers, interesting man, takes part in local cultural events...Jon Rogers, one of the most respected members of our community, begins to act strange...carries pencils in his hands and wanders around our clean suburb talking to himself about books he lost, plays he's searching for, almost poems, flying sentences, drooping images... *(He begins to smile, realizing he's overdramatizing a bit.)*... this won't do...too much like a soap...start again, slowly and sweetly this time...a smooth intro *(He prepares himself as if he is going on stage, coughs and then begins.)*...Mother, Father, I must leave you

66

and follow my craft. Writing calls... *(Breaks off, almost laughing.)*...
that's worse...there's a simpler way...just go do it, don't talk to yourself so much about writing...just say goodbye to them and write occasionally...if you've got the courage...Jon...you've got the courage
...don't I?... *(Walks off slowly.)*

After students have written monologues, it makes sense for them
to perform their work. It's also gratifying for students to have their
work performed by other students. It makes them feel like "real"
playwrights.

Dialogues

After developing monologues, it's good to introduce another
character and create a dialogue. The scene might change, the moment might precede or follow the monologue. But it is useful to
keep the first character and put that character with another (whose
character has been developed using the techniques described in
the monologue section). Stage dialogues can range from talk to
shouting matches. They are a form of action, integrated with movement and expression.

Conflict is at the basis of dialogue. This doesn't mean that all
dialogue is argument or insult. It means that the character's desires lead to conflict which lead to action (including dialogue).
This conflict (usually) gets resolved.

Here are some dialogues that can be used to introduce the exercise. Before introducing the dialogue, it makes sense to set the
scene of the piece used. For students to play out a dialogue with
conviction, it's important for them to think about where the characters are, how they feel, what they've done, and what they might
do in the future. Of course there are some dialogues that can stand
by themselves. The particular approach to introducing a dialogue
is really up to a teacher's sense of what will be effective with a particular group of students at a particular moment during the school
year.

The first two dialogues are for younger children:

1. *Heidi and Peter* by Hilary Clulow. This short dialogue between two girls (they could be boys or a boy and a girl) is about
generosity:

HEIDI: Are you very rich?

CLARA: Yes—I suppose I am—why do you ask?

HEIDI: Well...you see...I need a penny.

CLARA: A penny! Well of course I'll give you a penny—but why do you need it?

HEIDI: I promised the Hurdy-Gurdy boy that I'd give it to him.

CLARA: The Hurdy-Gurdy boy? What Hurdy-Gurdy boy?

HEIDI: The ragged little boy that plays the organ in the streets.

CLARA: But how did you get to know him?

HEIDI: Well you see I strayed off from Aunt Detie on the way here—that's why we were late—and a long way off I could see a tower with a golden shining ball on the top. I thought that if I could climb to the top of the tower I would be able to see my mountain and...maybe...my Grandfather's hut and...

CLARA: But how does the Hurdy-Gurdy boy come into this?

HEIDI: He showed me how to reach the tower. But he said that it would cost a penny. I knew you had lots of money—at least, that's what Aunt Detie said—so I thought you'd be able to spare the penny.

CLARA: Of course I'll give it to you Heidi. Do you want it now?

HEIDI: Oh no. The boy will call at the house for it. He's gone back to the tower for the kitten.

CLARA: The kitten?!

HEIDI: Yes—you see the tower is infested with mice and the keeper has dozens of cats. He was awfully kind to me and when I didn't even get a glimpse of my mountain when he took me right to the top of the tower, he promised to give me one of his kittens instead. It's the loveliest, fluffiest thing you've ever seen. I was certain you would like to have it.

2. *The Ugly Duckling* by A. A. Milne. This is a conversation between a prince and a princess about the beauty that lies beneath appearances.

PRINCESS: What fun. I love secrets...Well, here's mine. When I was born, one of my godmothers promised that I should be very beautiful.

PRINCE: How right she was.

PRINCESS: But the other one said this:

I give you with this kiss

A wedding-day surprise.

Where ignorance is bliss

'Tis folly to be wise.

And nobody knew what it meant. And I grew up very plain. And then, when I was about ten, I met my godmother in the forest one day. It was my tenth birthday. Nobody knows this—except you.

PRINCE: Except us.

PRINCESS: Except us. And she told me what her gift meant. It meant that I *was* beautiful—but everybody else was to go on being ignorant, and thinking me plain, until my wedding-day. Because, she said, she didn't want me to grow up spoilt and wilful and vain, as I should have done if everybody had always been saying how beautiful I was; and the best thing in the world, she said, was to be quite sure of yourself, but not to expect admiration from other people. So ever since then my mirror has told me I'm beautiful, and everybody else thinks me ugly, and I get a lot of fun out of it.

PRINCE: Well, seeing that Dulcibella is the result, I can only say that your godmother was very, very wise.

PRINCESS: And now tell me *your* secret.

The next three dialogue examples are for older children, and it is probably sensible to explain something about the whole play and the issues involved, either before doing the scenes or after students have tried them cold.

3. This is from John Steinbeck's *Of Mice and Men*. In this dialogue between Lennie, who is a kind, tall, and strong retarded person, and George, who has decided to give up some of his dreams to take care of Lennie, they talk about some of the bad situations Lennie has gotten them into. Lennie has innocently hurt people and animals, and George, who loves him, knows that Lenny does not understand the consequences of his strength or the nature of his actions.

LENNIE: Why ain't we goin' on the ranch to get some supper? They got supper at the ranch.

GEORGE: No reason at all. I just like it here. Tomorrow we'll be goin' to work. I seen thrashing machines on the way down; that means we'll be buckin' grain bags. Bustin' a gut liftin' up them bags. Tonight I'm gonna lay right here an' look up! Tonight there ain't a grain bag or a boss in the world. Tonight, the drinks is on the . . . house. Nice house we got here, Lennie.

LENNIE: *(Gets up on his knees and looks down at George, plaintively.)* Ain't we gonna have no supper?

GEORGE: Sure we are. You gather up some dead willow sticks. I got three cans of beans in my bindle. I'll open 'em up while you get a fire ready. We'll eat 'em cold.

LENNIE: *(Companionably.)* I like beans with ketchup.

GEORGE: Well, we ain't got no ketchup. You go get the wood, and don't you fool around none. Be dark before long. *(Lennie lumbers to his feet and disappears into the brush. George gets out the bean cans, opens two of them, suddenly turns his head and listens. A little sound of splashing comes from the direction that Lennie has taken. George looks after him; shakes his head. Lennie comes back carrying a few small willow sticks in his hand.)* All right, give me that mouse.

LENNIE: *(With elaborate pantomime of innocence.)* What, George? I ain't go no mouse.

GEORGE: *(Holding out his hand.)* Come on! Give it to me! You ain't puttin' nothing over. *(Lennie hesitates, backs away, turns and looks as if he were going to run. Coldly.)* You gonna give me that mouse or do I have to take a sock at you?

LENNIE: Give you what, George?

GEORGE: You know goddamn well, what! I want that mouse!

LENNIE: *(Almost in tears.)* I don't know why I can't keep it. It ain't no-body's mouse. I didn't steal it! I found it layin' right beside the road. *(George snaps his fingers sharply, and Lennie lays the mouse in his hand.)* I wasn't doin' nothing bad with it. Just stroking it. That ain't bad.

GEORGE: *(Stands up and throws the mouse as far as he can into the brush, then he steps to the pool, and washes his hands.)* You crazy fool! Thought you could get away with it, didn't you? Don't you think I could see your feet was wet where you went in the water to get it? *(Lennie whimpers like a puppy.)* Blubbering like a baby. Jesus Christ, a big guy like you! *(Lennie tries to control himself, but his lips quiver and his face works with effort. George puts his hand on Lennie's shoulder for a moment.)* Aw, Lennie, I ain't takin' it away just for meanness. That mouse ain't fresh. Besides, you broke it pettin' it. You get a mouse that's fresh and I'll let you keep it a little while.

LENNIE: I don't know where there is no other mouse. I remember a lady used to give 'em to me. Ever' one she got she used to give it to me, but that lady ain't here no more.

GEORGE: Lady, huh!. . . Give me them sticks there. . . . Don't even remember who that lady was. That was your own Aunt Clara. She stopped givin' 'em to you. You always killed 'em.

LENNIE: *(Sadly and apologetically.)* They was so little. I'd pet 'em and pretty soon they bit my fingers and then I pinched their head a little bit and then they was dead. . .because they was so little. I wish we'd get the rabbits pretty soon, George. They ain't so little.

4. This dialogue is from Arthur Miller's *Death of a Salesman*. It is the opening of the play. Willy Loman has come home from another unsuccessful business trip and is greeted by his wife. Willy is really depressed and his wife is worried about him. Willy is a failure in life, yet he and his family pretend that he is a marvelous salesman. The play opens as Willy's life begins to unravel and the truth begins to overwhelm his family. A way to introduce this might be to discuss the nature of failure and the things people do to hide it from themselves.

A melody is heard, played upon a flute. It is small and fine, telling of grass and trees and horizon. The curtain rises.

From the right, Willy Loman, the Salesman, enters, carrying two large sample cases. The flute plays on. He hears but is not aware of it. He is past sixty years of age, dressed quietly. Even as he crosses the stage to the doorway of the house, his exhaustion is apparent. He unlocks the door, comes into the kitchen, and thankfully lets his burden down, feeling the soreness of his palms. A word-sigh escapes his lips— it might be "Oh, boy, oh boy." He closes the door, then carries his cases out into the living-room, through the draped kitchen doorway.

Linda, his wife, has stirred in her bed at the right. She gets out and puts on a robe, listening. Most often jovial, she has developed an iron repression of her exceptions to Willy's behavior—she more than loves him, she admires him, as though his mercurial nature, his temper, his massive dreams and little cruelties, served her only as sharp reminders of the turbulent longings within him, longings which she shares but lacks the temperament to utter and follow to their end.

LINDA: *(hearing Willy outside the bedroom, calls with some trepidation)* Willy!

WILLY: It's all right. I came back.

LINDA: Why? What happened? *(Slight pause)* Did something happen, Willy?

WILLY: No, nothing happened.

LINDA: You didn't smash the car, did you?

WILLY: *(with casual irritation)* I said nothing happened. Didn't you hear me?

LINDA: Don't you feel well?

WILLY: I'm tired to the death. *(The flute has faded away. He sits on the bed beside her, a little numb)* I couldn't make it. I just couldn't make it, Linda.

LINDA: *(very carefully, delicately)* Where were you all day? You look terrible.

WILLY: I got as far as a little above Yonkers. I stopped for a cup of coffee. Maybe it was the coffee.

LINDA: What?

WILLY: *(after a pause)* I suddenly couldn't drive any more. The car kept going off onto the shoulder, y'know?

LINDA: *(helpfully)* Oh. Maybe it was the steering again. I don't think Angelo knows the Studebaker.

WILLY: No, it's me, it's me. Suddenly I realize I'm goin' sixty miles an hour and I don't remember the last five minutes. I'm—I can't seem to—keep my mind on it.

LINDA: Maybe it's your glasses. You never went for your new glasses.

WILLY: No, I see everything. I came back ten miles an hour. It took me nearly four hours from Yonkers.

LINDA: *(resigned)* Well, you'll just have to take a rest, Willy, you can't continue this way.

WILLY: I just got back from Florida.

LINDA: But you didn't rest your mind. Your mind is overactive and the mind is what counts, dear.

WILLY: I'll start out in the morning. Maybe I'll feel better in the morning. *(She is taking off his shoes)* These goddamn arch supports are killing me.

LINDA: Take an aspirin. Should I get you an aspirin? It'll soothe you.

WILLY: *(with wonder)* I was driving along, you understand? And I was fine. I was even observing the scenery. You can imagine, me looking at scenery, on the road every week of my life. But it's so beautiful up there, Linda, the trees are so thick, and the sun is warm. I opened the windshield and just let the warm air bathe over me. And then all of a sudden I'm goin' off the road! I'm tellin' ya, I absolutely forgot I was driving. If I'd've gone the other way over the white line I might've killed somebody. So I went on again—and five minutes later I'm dreamin' again, and I nearly—*(He presses two fingers against his eyes)* I have such thoughts, I have such strange thoughts.

LINDA: Willy, dear. Talk to them again. There's no reason why you can't work in New York.

WILLY: They don't need me in New York. I'm the New England man. I'm vital in New England.

LINDA: But you're sixty years old. They can't expect you to keep traveling every week.

WILLY: I'll have to send a wire to Portland. I'm supposed to see Brown and Morrison tomorrow morning at ten o'clock to show the line. Goddammit, I could sell them! *(He starts putting on his jacket)*

LINDA: *(taking the jacket from him)* Why don't you go down to the place tomorrow and tell Howard you've simply got to work in New York? You're too accommodating, dear.

WILLY: If old man Wagner was alive I'd a been in charge of New York now! That man was a prince, he was a masterful man. But that boy of his, that Howard, he don't appreciate. When I went north the first time, the Wagner Company didn't know where New England was!

LINDA: Why don't you tell those things to Howard, dear?

WILLY: *(encouraged)* I will, I definitely will. Is there any cheese?

LINDA: I'll make you a sandwich.

WILLY: No, go to sleep. I'll take some milk. I'll be up right away. The boys in?

LINDA: They're sleeping. Happy took Biff on a date tonight.

WILLY: *(interested)* That so?

LINDA: It was so nice to see them shaving together, one behind the other, in the bathroom. And going out together. You notice? The whole house smells of shaving lotion.

WILLY: Figure it out. Work a lifetime to pay off a house. You finally own it, and there's nobody to live in it.

LINDA: Well, dear, life is a casting off. It's always that way.

WILLY: No, no, some people — some people accomplish something. Did Biff say anything after I went this morning?

LINDA: You shouldn't have criticized him, Willy, especially after he just got off the train. You mustn't lose your temper with him.

WILLY: When the hell did I lose my temper? I simply asked him if he was making any money. Is that a criticism?

LINDA: But, dear, how could he make any money?

WILLY: *(worried and angered)* There's such an undercurrent in him. He became a moody man. Did he apologize when I left this morning?

LINDA: He was crestfallen, Willy. You know how he admires you. I think if he finds himself, then you'll both be happier and not fight any more.

WILLY: How can he find himself on a farm? Is that a life? A farmhand? In the beginning, when he was young, I thought, well, a young man, it's good for him to tramp around, take a lot of different jobs. But it's more than ten years now and he has yet to make thirty-five dollars a week!

LINDA: He's finding himself, Willy.

WILLY: Not finding yourself at the age of thirty-four is a disgrace!

LINDA: Shh!

WILLY: The trouble is he's lazy, goddammit!

LINDA: Willy, please!

WILLY: Biff is a lazy bum!

LINDA: They're sleeping. Get something to eat. Go on down.

WILLY: Why did he come home? I would like to know what brought him home.

LINDA: I don't know. I think he's still lost, Willy. I think he's very lost.

WILLY: Biff Loman is lost. In the greatest country in the world a young man with such — personal attractiveness, gets lost. And such a hard worker. There's one thing about Biff — he's not lazy.

LINDA: Never.

WILLY: *(with pity and resolve)* I'll see him in the morning; I'll have a nice talk with him. I'll get him a job selling. He could be big in no time. My God! Remember how they used to follow him around in high school? When he smiled at one of them their faces lit up. When he walked down the street. . . *(He loses himself in reminiscences)*

5. This last dialogue, between a husband and a wife, is from Henrik Ibsen's *A Doll's House*. Nora, the wife, has decided to leave her husband. This dialogue is about a woman liberating herself from the image of being a man's doll and plaything:

NORA: I've never felt as convinced and as lucid as I am tonight.

HELMER: You're convinced and lucid and you're abandoning your husband and children. . .

NORA: Yes. That's right.

HELMER: Then there's only one possible explanation.

NORA: What's that?

HELMER: You don't love me any more.

NORA: That's exactly it.

HELMER: Nora!. . .How can you say that?

NORA: It hurts me very much to say it, Torvald, you've always been so kind to me. But there's nothing I can do about it. I don't love you any more.

HELMER: *(Making an effort to be calm.)* And you've thought about this and you're quite sure?

NORA: Absolutely positive. That's why I don't want to stay here any more.

HELMER: Can you explain to me why it is I've lost your love?

NORA: Yes, I can. It was this evening, when the miracle didn't happen. That's when I realized you weren't the man I thought you were.

HELMER: Can't you be a bit more explicit? I don't understand.

NORA: I've waited so patiently, eight years now. God, I knew well enough you can't expect miracles to happen every day. But when this terrible storm broke over me, I was sure it couldn't fail to come: the miracle. While Krogstad's letter was lying out there, it never occurred to me for a minute that you could possibly give in to his conditions. I was sure you were bound to say tell the whole world if you want to. And once that had happened...

HELMER: You mean you think I should have let my own wife be exposed to shame and disgrace...?

NORA: Once that had happened I was sure you were bound to step forward and take all the blame yourself and say, I'm the guilty one.

HELMER. Nora...!

NORA: You mean I would never have let you make a sacrifice like that? No, of course I wouldn't. But what could I have done? It would have been my word against yours.... *That* was the miracle I was hoping for in my misery. And it was to prevent *that* that I wanted to kill myself.

HELMER: I'd gladly work day and night for you, Nora...put up with any suffering or hardship for your sake. But no one would sacrifice his honor, even for love.

NORA: Millions of women have.

HELMER: You think and talk like an ignorant child.

NORA: Maybe. But you don't think or talk like the man I want to spend my life with. When you stopped being terrified—not about what threatened me, but about your own reputation—once you had nothing more to fear, then, as far as you were concerned, it was as if the whole thing had never happened. Everything was exactly as before, I was your little lark, your doll, from now on you'd be doubly careful looking after me, because I was so frail and delicate.... *(Stands up.)* At that moment, Torvald, I realized that I'd been living with a stranger for eight years, and that I'd had three children by him....I can't bear to think about it! I could tear myself to pieces.

HELMER: *(Sadly.)* I see. I see. A chasm has opened up between us.... Isn't...isn't there any way we could bridge it, Nora?

NORA: The way I am now, I'm no sort of a wife for you.

HELMER: I'm strong enough to change.

NORA: Perhaps...if your doll is taken away from you.

HELMER: To be separated...separated from you. No, Nora, I just can't grasp the idea.

NORA: *(Going into the room on the R.)* All the more reason for it to happen.

Dialogues add a new element to performance. Since there is more than one character involved, the author needs to act with someone else or direct two other actors. Directing is wonderful experience because it gives an author the opportunity to experience how a work plays in the hands of others. It can lead to revision and reformulation. Actually, the best way I know to work with dialogues and scenes is to have the author direct and collaborate with the actors in revising and improving the work.

Scenes:
Turning Stories into Monologues, Dialogues, and Conversations among Any Number of People

I have found very few interesting plays written for young people. Most of them tend to be boring and antiseptic, a bit like the stories in *Archie* comics, though not as funny. However, children's *books* are full of the complexities and wonders of human experience. One way to get material for doing theater is to create dramatic scenes out of dialogues in books. I've done it a lot, but the most fun is having students find a favorite conversation in a book they love and have them turn it into a short monologue, dialogue, or scene. Here are two partially adapted selections. With your students, you might want to complete the adaptations and perform them for the class.

The first text is the beginning of Louisa May Alcott's *Little Women*. The characters are four sisters, Meg, Jo, Beth, and Amy. The time is the Civil War. Before beginning the adaptation, it might be useful to read and discuss the selection with your students.

"Christmas won't be Christmas without any presents," grumbled Jo, lying on the rug.

"It's so dreadful to be poor!" sighed Meg, looking down at her old dress.

"I don't think it's fair for some girls to have plenty of pretty things, and other girls nothing at all," added little Amy, with an injured sniff.

"We've got father and mother and each other," said Beth contentedly, from her corner.

The four young faces on which the firelight shone brightened at the cheerful words, but darkened again as Jo said sadly,—

"We haven't got father, and shall not have him for a long time." She didn't say "Perhaps never," but each silently added it, thinking of father far away, where the fighting was.

Nobody spoke for a minute; then Meg said in an altered tone,—

"You know the reason mother proposed not having any presents this Christmas was because it is going to be a hard winter for every one; and she thinks we ought not to spend money for pleasure, when our men are suffering so in the army. We can't do much, but we can make our little sacrifices, and ought to do it gladly. But I am afraid I don't;" and Meg shook her head, as she thought regretfully of all the pretty things she wanted.

"But I don't think the little we should spend would do any good. We've each got a dollar, and the army wouldn't be much helped by our giving that. I agree not to expect anything from mother or you, but I do want to buy Undine and Sintram for myself; I've wanted it *so* long," said Jo, who was a bookworm.

"I have planned to spend mine in new music," said Beth, with a little sigh, which no one heard but the hearth-brush and kettle-holder.

"I shall get a nice box of Faber's drawing-pencils; I really need them," said Amy decidedly.

"Mother didn't say anything about our money, and she won't wish us to give up everything. Let's each buy what we want, and have a little fun; I'm sure we work hard enough to earn it," cried Jo, examining the heels of her shoes in a gentlemanly manner.

"I know *I* do,—teaching those tiresome children nearly all day, when I'm longing to enjoy myself at home," began Meg, in the complaining tone again.

"You don't have half such a hard time as I do," said Jo. "How would you like to be shut up for hours with a nervous, fussy old lady, who keeps you trotting, is never satisfied, and worries you till you're ready to fly out of the window or cry?"

"It's naughty to fret; but I do think washing dishes and keeping things tidy is the worst work in the world. It makes me cross; and my hands get so stiff, I can't practice well at all;" and Beth looked at her rough hands with a sigh that any one could hear that time.

"I don't believe any of you suffer as I do," cried Amy; "for you don't have to go to school with impertinent girls, who plague you if you don't know your lessons, and laugh at your dressers, and label your father if he isn't rich, and insult you when your nose isn't nice."

"If you mean *libel*, I'd say so, and not talk about *labels*, as if papa was a pickle-bottle," advised Jo, laughing.

"I know what I mean, and you needn't be *statirical* about it. It's proper to use good words, and improve your *vocabilary*," returned Amy, with dignity.

"Don't peck at one another, children. Don't you wish we had the money papa lost when we were little, Jo? Dear me! how happy and good we'd be, if we had no worries!" said Meg, who could remember better times.

"You said, the other day, you thought we were a deal happier than the King children, for they were fighting and fretting all the time, in spite of their money."

"So I did, Beth. Well, I think we are; for, though we do have to work, we make fun for ourselves, and are a pretty jolly set, as Jo would say."

"Jo does use such slang words!" observed Amy, with a reproving look at the long figure stretched on the rug. Jo immediately sat up, put her hands in her pockets, and began to whistle.

"Don't, Jo; it's so boyish!"

"That's why I do it."

"I detest rude, unlady-like girls!"

"I hate affected, niminy-piminy chits!"

"'Birds in their little nests agree,'" sang Beth, the peacemaker, with such a funny face that both sharp voices softened to a laugh, and the "pecking" ended for that time.

"Really, girls, you are both to be blamed," said Meg, beginning to lecture in her elder-sisterly fashion. "You are old enough to leave off boyish tricks, and to behave better, Josephine. It didn't matter so much when you were a little girl; but now you are so tall, and turn up your hair, you should remember that you are a young lady."

"I'm not! And if turning up my hair makes me one, I'll wear it in two tails till I'm twenty," cried Jo, pulling off her net, and shaking down a chestnut mane. "I hate to think I've got to grow up, and be Miss March, and wear long gowns, and look as prim as a China-aster! It's bad enough to be a girl anyway, when I like boys' games and work and manners! I can't get over my disappointment in not being a boy; and it's worse than ever now, for I'm dying to go and fight with papa, and I can only stay at home and knit, like a poky old woman!" And Jo shook the blue army-sock till the needles rattled like castanets, and her ball bounded across the room.

"Poor Jo! It's too bad, but it can't be helped; so you must try to be contented with making your name boyish, and playing brother to us girls," said Beth, stroking the rough head at her knee with a hand that all the dish-washing and dusting in the world could not make ungentle in its touch.

"As for you, Amy," continued Meg, "you are altogether too particular and prim. Your airs are funny now; but you'll grow up an affected little goose, if you don't take care. I like your nice manners and refined ways of speaking, when you don't try to be elegant; but your absurd words are as bad as Jo's slang."

"If Jo is a tom-boy and Amy a goose, what am I, please?" asked Beth, ready to share the lecture.

"You're a dear, and nothing else," answered Meg warmly; and no one contradicted her, for the "Mouse" was the pet of the family.

As young readers like to know "how people look," we will take this moment to give them a little sketch of the four sisters, who sat knitting away in the twilight, while the December snow fell quietly without, and the fire crackled cheerfully within. It was a comfortable old room, though the carpet was faded and the furniture very plain; for a good picture or two hung on the walls, books filled the recesses, chrysanthemums and Christmas roses bloomed in the windows, and a pleasant atmosphere of home-peace pervaded it.

Margaret, the eldest of the four, was sixteen, and very pretty, being plump and fair, with large eyes, plenty of soft, brown hair, a sweet mouth, and white hands, of which she was rather vain. Fifteen-year-old Jo was very tall, thin, and brown, and reminded one of a colt; for she never seemed to know what to do with her long limbs, which were very much in her way. She had a decided mouth, a comical nose, and sharp, gray eyes, which appeared to see everything, and were by turns fierce, funny, or thoughtful. Her long, thick hair was her one beauty; but it was usually bundled into a net, to be out of her way. Round shoulders had Jo, big hands and feet, a fly-away look to her clothes, and the uncomfortable appearance of a girl who was rapidly shooting up into a woman, and didn't like it. Elizabeth—or Beth, as every one called her — was a rosy, smooth-haired, bright-eyed girl of thirteen, with a shy manner, a timid voice, and a peaceful expression, which was seldom disturbed. Her father called her "Little Tranquility," and the name suited her excellently; for she seemed to live in a happy world of her own, only venturing out to meet the few whom she trusted and loved. Amy, though the youngest, was a most important person,—in her own opinion at least. A regular snow-maiden, with blue eyes, and yellow hair, curling on her shoulders, pale and slender, and always carrying herself like a young lady mindful of her manners. What the characters of the four sisters were we will leave to be found out.

The clock struck six; and, having swept up the hearth, Beth put a pair of slippers down to warm. Somehow the sight of the old shoes had a good effect upon the girls; for mother was coming, and every one brightened to welcome her. Meg stopped lecturing, and lighted the lamp, Amy got out of the easy-chair without being asked, and Jo forgot how tired she was as she sat up to hold the slippers nearer to the blaze.

"They are quite worn out; Marmee must have a new pair."

"I thought I'd get her some with my dollar," said Beth.

"No, I shall!" cried Amy.

"I'm the oldest," began Meg, but Jo cut in with a decided—

"I'm the man of the family now papa is away, and *I* shall provide the slippers, for he told me to take special care of mother while he was gone."

"I'll tell you what we'll do," said Beth; "let's each get her something for Christmas, and not get anything for ourselves."

"That's like you, dear! What will we get?" exclaimed Jo.

Here is an adaptation of the beginning of the selection:

Setting: It is Christmas eve and the four sisters are sitting around the fireplace.
JO: Christmas won't be Christmas without any presents. . . .
MEG: It's so dreadful to be poor.
AMY: I don't think it's fair for some girls to have plenty of pretty things and other girls nothing at all.
BETH: We've got mother and father and each other.
JO: We haven't got father, and shall not have him for a long time.
MEG: You know the reason mother proposed not having any presents this Christmas was because it is going to be a hard winter for everyone; and she thinks we ought not to spend money for pleasure, when our men are suffering so in the army. We can't do much, but can make little sacrifices, and ought to do it gladly. But I am afraid I don't.

The second selection is the chapter from *Pippi Longstocking* entitled "Pippi Entertains Two Burglars." Two tramps, Bloom and Thunder-Karlsson, knock on Pippi's door. They are up to no good. Pippi is sitting at the table counting out her gold pieces, and her monkey Nilsson is asleep in a cradle. The tramps don't know what they're getting into:

One dark autumn evening two tramps came walking down the road past Villa Villekulla. They were two bad thieves wandering about the country to see what they could steal. They saw that there was a light in the windows of Villa Villekulla and decided to go in to ask for a sandwich.

That evening Pippi had poured out all her gold pieces on the kitchen floor and sat there counting them. To be sure, she couldn't count very well, but she did it now and then anyway, just to keep everything in order.

". . . sixty-five, sixty-six, sixty-seven, sixty-eight, sixty-nine, sixty-ten, sixty-eleven, sixty-twelve, sixty-thirteen, sixty-sixteen—whew, it makes my throat feel like sixty! Goodness, there must be *some* more numbers in the arithmetic—oh, yes, now I remember—one hundred four, one thousand. That certainly is a lot of money," said Pippi.

There was a loud knock on the door.

"Walk in or stay out, whichever you choose!" shouted Pippi. "I never force anyone against his will."

The door opened and the two tramps came in. You can imagine that they opened their eyes when they saw a little red-headed girl sitting all alone on the floor, counting money.

"Are you all alone at home?" they asked craftily.

"Of course not," said Pippi. "Mr. Nilsson is at home too."

The thieves couldn't very well know that Mr. Nilsson was a monkey sleeping in a little green bed with a doll's quilt around his stomach. They thought the man of the house must be named Mr. Nilsson and they winked at each other. "We can come back a little later" is what they meant, but to Pippi they said, "We just came in to ask what your clock is."

They were so excited that they had forgotten all about the sandwich.

"Great, strong men who don't know what a clock is!" said Pippi. "Where in the world were you brought up? The clock is a little round thingamajig that says 'tick tack, tick tack,' and that goes and goes but never gets to the door. Do you know any more riddles? Out with them if you do," said Pippi encouragingly.

The tramps thought Pippi was too little to tell time, so without another word they went out again.

"I don't demand that you say 'tack'" [thanks in Swedish], shouted Pippi after them, "but you could at least make an effort to say 'tick.' You haven't even as much sense as a clock has. But by all means go in peace." And Pippi went back to her counting.

No sooner were the tramps outside than they began to rub their hands with delight. "Did you see all that money? Heavenly day!" said one of them.

"Yes, once in a while luck is with us," said the other. "All we need to do is wait until the kid and that Nilsson are asleep. Then we'll sneak in and grab the dough."

They sat down under an oak tree in the garden to wait. A drizzling rain was falling; they were very hungry, so they were quite uncomfortable, but the thought of all that money kept their spirits up.

From time to time lights went out in other houses, but in Villa Villekulla they shone on. It so happened that Pippi was learning to dance the schottische, and she didn't want to go to bed until she was sure she could do it. At last, however, the lights went out in the windows of Villa Villekulla too.

The tramps waited quite a while until they were sure Mr. Nilsson would have gone to sleep. At last they crept quietly up to the kitchen door and prepared to open it with their burglar tools. Meanwhile one of them—his name, as a matter of fact, was Bloom—just happened to feel the doorknob. The door was not locked!

"Well, some people *are* smart!" he whispered to his companion. "The door is open!"

"So much the better for us," answered his companion, a black-haired man called Thunder-Karlsson by those who knew him. Thunder-Karlsson turned on his pocket flashlight, and they crept into the kitchen. There was no one there. In the next room was Pippi's bed, and there also stood Mr. Nilsson's little doll bed.

Thunder-Karlsson opened the door and looked around carefully. Everything was quiet as he played his flashlight around the room. When the light touched Pippi's bed the two tramps were amazed to see nothing but a pair of feet on the pillow. Pippi, as usual, had her head under the covers at the foot of the bed.

"That must be the girl," whispered Thunder-Karlsson to Bloom. "And no doubt she sleeps soundly. But where in the world is Nilsson, do you suppose?"

"*Mr.* Nilsson, if you please," came Pippi's calm voice from under the covers. "*Mr.* Nilsson is in the little green doll bed."

The tramps were so startled that they almost rushed out at once, but then it suddenly dawned on them what Pippi had said. That Mr. Nilsson was lying in a *doll's* bed! And now in the light of the flashlight they could see the little bed and the tiny monkey lying in it.

Thunder-Karlsson couldn't help laughing. "Bloom," he said, "Mr. Nilsson is a monkey. Can you beat that?"

"Well, what did you think he was?" came Pippi's calm voice from under the covers again. "A lawn mower?"

"Aren't your mother and father at home?" asked Bloom.

"No," said Pippi. "They're gone. Completely gone."

Thunder-Karlsson and Bloom chuckled with delight.

"Listen, little girl," said Thunder-Karlsson, "come out so we can talk to you."

"No, I'm sleeping," said Pippi. "Is it more riddles you want? If so, answer this one. What is it that goes and goes and never gets to the door?"

Now Bloom went over and pulled the covers off Pippi.

"Can you dance the schottische?" asked Pippi, looking at him gravely in the eye. "I can."

"You ask too many questions," said Thunder-Karlsson. "Can we ask a few too? Where, for instance, is the money you had on the floor a little while ago?"

"In the suitcase on top of the wardrobe," answered Pippi truthfully. Thunder-Karlsson and Bloom grinned.

"I hope you don't have anything against our taking it, little friend," said Thunder-Karlsson.

"Certainly not," said Pippi. "Of course I don't."

Whereupon Bloom lifted down the suitcase.

"I hope you don't have anything against my taking it back, little friend," said Pippi, getting out of bed and stepping over to Bloom.

Bloom had no idea how it all happened, but suddenly the suitcase was in Pippi's hand.

"Here, quit your fooling!" said Thunder-Karlsson angrily. "Hand over the suitcase." He took Pippi firmly by the hand and tried to snatch back the booty.

"Fooling, fooling, too much fooling," said Pippi and lifted Thunder-Karlsson up on the wardrobe. A moment later she had Bloom up there too. Then the tramps were frightened; they began to see that Pippi was no ordinary girl. However, the suitcase tempted them so much they forgot their fright.

"Come on now, both together," yelled Thunder-Karlsson, and they jumped down from the wardrobe and threw themselves on Pippi, who had the suitcase in her hand. Pippi gave each one a little poke with her finger, and they shrank away into a corner. Before they had a chance to get up again, Pippi had fetched a rope and quick as a flash had bound the arms and legs of both burglars. Now they sang a different tune.

"Please, please, miss," begged Thunder-Karlsson, "forgive us. We were only joking. Don't hurt us. We are just two tramps who came in to ask for food."

Bloom even began to cry a bit.

Pippi put the suitcase neatly back on the wardrobe. Then she turned to her prisoners. "Can either of you dance the schottische?"

"Why, yes," said Thunder-Karlsson, "I guess we both can."

"Oh, what fun!" cried Pippi, clapping her hands. "Can't we dance a little? I've just learned, you know."

"Well, certainly, by all means," said Thunder-Karlsson, a bit confused.

Pippi took some large scissors and cut the ropes that bound her guests.

"But we don't have any music," she said in a worried voice. Then she had an idea. "Can't you blow on a comb?" she said to Bloom. "And I'll dance with him." She pointed to Thunder-Karlsson.

Oh, yes, Bloom could blow on a comb, all right. And blow he did, so that you could hear it all through the house. Mr. Nilsson sat up in bed, wide awake, just in time to see Pippi whirling around with Thunder-Karlsson. She was dead serious and danced as if her life depended on it.

At last Bloom said he couldn't blow on the comb any longer because it tickled his mouth unmercifully. And Thunder-Karlsson, who had tramped the roads all day, began to feel tired.

"Oh, please, just a little longer," begged Pippi, dancing on, and Bloom and Thunder-Karlsson could do nothing but continue.

At three in the morning Pippi said, "I could keep on dancing until Thursday, but maybe you're tired and hungry."

That was exactly what they were, though they hardly dared to say so. Pippi went to the pantry and took out bread and cheese and butter, ham and cold roast and milk; and they sat around the kitchen table—Bloom and Thunder-Karlsson and Pippi—and ate until they were almost four-cornered.

Pippi poured a little milk into her ear. "That's good for earache," she said.

"Poor thing, have you got an earache?" asked Bloom.

"No," said Pippi, "but I might get one."

Finally the two tramps got up, thanked Pippi for the food, and begged to be allowed to say good-by.

"It was awfully jolly that you came. Do you really have to go so soon?" said Pippi regretfully. "Never have I seen anyone who can dance the schottische the way you do, my sugar pig," she said to Thunder-Karlsson. And to Bloom, "If you keep on practicing on the comb, you won't notice the tickling."

As they were going out of the door Pippi came running after them and gave them each a gold piece. "These you have honestly earned," she said.

Here is the beginning of a stage rendition of the Pippi and the burglars episode.

Setting: Pippi is sitting at the table counting her gold pieces. There is a knock on the door.

PIPPI: Sixty-five, sixty-six, sixty-seven, sixty-eight, sixty-nine, sixty-ten, sixty-eleven, sixty-twelve, sixty-thirteen, sixty-sixteen — whew, it makes my throat feel like sixty! Goodness there must be some more numbers in the arithmetic — oh, yes, now I remember — one hundred four, one thousand. That certainly is a lot of money. *(There's a knock on the door.)* Walk in or stay out. I never force anyone against his will.

BLOOM and THUNDER-KARLSSON *(together)*: Are you all alone at home?

PIPPI: Of course not, Mr. Nilsson is at home too.

BLOOM and THUNDER-KARLSSON *(together)*: We just came in to ask what your clock is.

PIPPI: Great! Strong men who don't know what a clock is. Where in the world were you brought up?

Chapter 4
Adapting Plays for Performance

Going from improvisation and the development of monologues and dialogues to the production of a whole play requires a focused commitment to a specific performance. When you make this move it is important to choose a play you love, or at least one that does not bore you, since producing a play takes a lot of patience and involves considerable frustration. Even the most outgoing and confident children get nervous when they prepare to perform in public. And the number of details one has to keep in mind can distract the most organized and confident teacher. This might seem obvious, yet many teachers have plays they don't like forced on them by rigid curricula and by imagined community standards, and plays they love censored as unfit for performance by young people. Of course, the "unfit" designation doesn't have to do with the students. It has to do with administrative worries about what the parents and the community will think. Serious confrontations with important issues are not usually welcome in the classroom. Unfortunately, doing drama in schools is not as free as doing drama in more independent settings, such as community or teen centers.

In adapting a play, the first step is to choose a play to invest time, energy, and emotion in. There are at least two ways to do this. One is to decide upon the theme you want the play to express. The other is to start with a play and dig the themes out of it. I've tried both ways.

Several years ago my wife and I ran a two-week summer camp for about forty local children who were from seven to fourteen

86

years old. The camp was held at our home, which also doubles as an education center. We have eleven acres and, with the help of friends, have built an outdoor stage. The stage is set in the woods, a wonderful place for pageants and large plays, but hopeless for intimate theater. For our first camp, I looked for a play that could involve all of the children, that had plenty of action, and that embodied a theme that would engage everybody's interest. I was fortunate enough to have Sande Zeig, a mime, actress, and playwright, working with me. We decided upon the theme of female defiance of male authority. The Greek tragedy *Antigone* seemed to fit what we hoped to dramatize; that is, the kinds of decisions men and women have to face when there is a struggle over established male authority and the main opposition comes from women.

Here's the *Oxford Companion to Classical Literatures* entry for Antigone:

Antigone, a tragedy by Sophocles, of unknown date, probably an early work.

Creon, ruler of Thebes, has forbidden on pain of death the burial of the body of Polynices (see *Oedipus*). Antigone resolves to defy the outrageous edict and perform the funeral rites for her brother. She is caught doing this and brought before the infuriated king. She justifies her act as in accordance with the overriding laws of the gods. Creon, unrelenting, condemns her to be immured alive in a cave. Her sister, Ismene, who has refused to share in her defiant act, now claims a share in her guilt and in her penalty, but is treated by Creon as demented. Haemon, Creon's son, betrothed to Antigone, pleads in vain with Creon. He goes out, warning his father that he will die with her. The seer Tiresias threatens Creon with the fearful consequences of his defiance of the divine laws. Creon, at last moved, sets out hurriedly for the cave where Antigone has been immured. He finds Haemon clasping her dead body, for Antigone has hanged herself. Haemon thrusts at Creon with his sword, but misses him, and then kills himself. Creon returns to the palace, to find that Eurydice, his wife, in despair has taken her own life.

On one of the first days of camp, I told the story of Antigone to the children. (The camp was so short that there was no time to read the original text through with the children.) I found that my description of the plot confused them. They didn't know why Antigone's brothers were fighting each other and why not being buried was such a big deal. The names of the characters were confusing. The nature of Greek tragedy, as well as its context, was totally unfamiliar to them.

That night, I decided to refresh myself on the background of the play, and to approach *Antigone* in the larger context of the tragedy of her father Oedipus, and that of the relationship between people and the gods in Ancient Greece. The next day I began by introducing Zeus, Hera, Athena, Hermes, and Poseidon as a bunch of querulous, silly gods who differed from people only in their immortality. We did improvisations based on the idea that no matter how much the gods argued, they simply could not kill each other. Sande turned the god improvisations into a clown show, as if the gods were nothing but a bunch of clowns commenting on the more serious and measured tragedies of mortals.

The younger children at the camp loved the god-clowns and Sande worked with them developing a clown show as I took the older children aside and explained to them the story of Oedipus, the role of the blind prophet Tiresias, and the Sphinx's riddle. I also explained the tragedies Oedipus and his children faced. Then I told the story of the death of Antigone's brothers and asked for volunteers to improvise Antigone, her sister Ismene, King Creon, his son Haemon, and the dead bodies of Antigone and Ismene's two brothers. The two bodies were laid on the stage, one with a flag draped around it and the other on a mound of twigs and redwood branches. One brother was honored and the other dishonored and the theme of the improvisation was for Antigone and Ismene to plead for a proper burial for both brothers.

During one improvisation, the king ordered the two sisters killed and his son agreed and helped him do it. During another the son refused. We worked through a number of variations before deciding upon the final form of the play.

As always, I kept notes on the improvisations, and based the final script of the play on the students' preferences. The script might go through a half a dozen to ten revisions in the course of developing it for performance.

Our play emerged from our conversations and improvisations involving the family of Oedipus. Following the general outlines of the story, I wrote a script that combined the original play with the choices students made in rendering their parts. Queen Jocasta, for example, became a powerful and militant figure even though she did not figure that strongly in the original story. The kids also wanted an onstage fight, a good bloody swordfight.

Blood and battle are central to classical theater and there is no point in retreating from them. In fact, it can be fun to include them. *Antigone* is a pretty bloody story and the kids loved that aspect of it as much as they did the feminist implications. Because of that I decided to teach classes in stage swordfighting. The play had to have choreographed fights, not bloody battles. We began swordfighting in slow motion and I made sure to be the guardian of the weapons. No free fighting was allowed. To my surprise the kids loved to thrust and parry in slow motion, to do swordfighting as ballet.

Once students got the hang of basic sword moves, I increased the speed of fighting until we got to an intense and convincing battle pace. Antigone, Ismene, and Jocasta insisted upon swordfighting and, not surprisingly, turned out to be as effective as Etocles, Polynices, Haemon and Creon. In a way, the message of the play was worked out through the swordfighting. On our stage battlefield the females could and often did outdo the males.

If you have never done any swordfighting, start with simple thrusts and parries, in slow motion. Use boffers, cardboard tubes, or some other safe material. In camp I taught swordfighting formally and refused to allow any stage fighting until a student passed a swordfighting test, which consisted of thrusting and parrying with me in the sense of dance and not in the sense of battle. Whoever passed the test got a fancy swordfighting license.

We had a number of things going on simultaneously. We had swordfighting, the god-clown show improvisations, and the rehearsal of the main characters in their tragic roles. At summer camp, we had a number of adults and high school students, each of whom could work with a small group of students; in the classroom, I use parent volunteers or high school aides, and often let students work independently in small groups.

After the play was cast, it was apparent that a number of the older girls lacked roles. This meant (as it usually does for me) finding new characters to fit into the play. Initially, I had planned upon a single narrator to help tie the action together (and therefore play the same role as the narrator did in our production of *The Four*

Alices), but instead I decided to split the narrator into seven parts. Since there were seven children without roles and the Muses numbered nine, I chose seven of the nine and the narration came from the Muses.

Here is a description of the Muses taken from the *Funk and Wagnalls Standard Dictionary of Folklore, Mythology and Legend*, edited by Maria Leach, which is an indispensable tool for teachers:

Muses In ancient Greek mythology, the nine (originally three) nymphs, daughters of Zeus and Mnemosyne, who presided over poetry and the arts of music. They had as their favorite dwelling-places Pieria near Olympus, their birthplace, Mt. Helicon and the springs Hippocrene and Aganippe, Mt. Parnassus, and Castalia. All these sites were sacred to the Muses. Later poets and mythographers felt it necessary to assign various fields of interest to each of the nine, but agreement is generally lacking. The Muses, and their most accepted provinces, are: Calliope—epic or heroic poetry; Clio—history or lyre-playing; Melpomene—tragedy or lyre-playing; Euterpe—tragedy, flute-playing, or lyric poetry; Erato—love poetry, hymns, lyre-playing, or pantomime; Terpsichore—choral dancing and singing or flute-playing; Urania—astronomy (i.e. cosmological poetry); Thalia—comedy or idyll; Polymnia (Polyhymnia)—hymns, pantomime, or religious dance.

As can be seen, the same field is often attributed to several Muses. There is no doubt however that as a group they presided over poetry. Several times they had contests with human or semi-divine beings, but the Muses always won. Thamyris lost to them, betting his enjoying each of them against whatever they cared to do to him; they blinded him and broke his lyre. Thamyris in Hades, blind and sitting by his useless instrument, was a favorite poetic and artistic example of punishment in the underworld. The Sphinx that terrified Thebes was given her riddle by the Muses.

Since there were originally three Muses and later nine, and because the Muses gave the Sphinx her riddle, I felt confident that using only seven of the Muses in our version of *Antigone* was in the spirit of Greek mythology. The Muses played the role of the traditional Greek chorus, the two parts of which commented on and sometimes argued about the action of the play. One set of Muses was on the left of the action, the other on the right.

All of the children were cast, and we spent a week and a half rehearsing the play in parts. The Muses would do their narratives; the gods their clown show; and the family of Oedipus the major dramatic story.

The biggest problem with doing plays this way is to give everyone a sense of the whole performance and to get them to know where they fit in. I tried, over and over, to go through the whole story, but without enough success. The dress rehearsal, which took place the day before we performed, was the first time the kids had the experience of being in a whole play, and that was too late. Since that first attempt at a classical play on a fairly large scale, I've written storyboards and outlines that all the students could see, as the rehearsals developed. I borrowed the use of storyboards from filmmaking, where a movie is drawn scene-by-scene on a pad that has a space for a sketch and a verbal description of the action. Even though storyboards are not usually used in the theater, I find them convenient for clarifying the development of an improvised play.

In appendix B is the script we finally came up with (see the illustrations section for pictures taken at our performance). The script developed from the improvisations and a lot of discussions among Sande, me, and all of the other people working on the play. The contribution of the student actors was substantial.

We had one performance in front of friends and parents, and then had a potluck dinner. The play was for us, not posterity.

With *Antigone*, I began with a theme, that of female defiance of male authority, and then selected a play. In the case of *The Tempest*, which I intend to do sometime during the next year, the play came first. This means that no matter how the play may emerge in collaboration with the cast, there is Shakespeare's script to work from.

I chose *The Tempest* because I love the play and because it embodies a number of themes I think young people will find compelling. Some of them are:

• Shipwreck and awakening in a world governed by magic
• A monster and a fairy who are enslaved through enchantment
• Young love

- Vengeance and forgiveness
- Wizardry
- Foolishness in the midst of serious business

The problem is how to move from Shakespeare's play to your own version of it in a manner that is consistent with the substance of the original, all done with spirit and joy. This means using as much of the language and plot of Shakespeare as students can master without having them become bored and mechanical on stage.

There is no best way to go about introducing *The Tempest* or any complex play. The cast of the play can range from six to seventeen in age and therefore I have to plan for differing perspectives on the plot and the language. The range in age can be a problem, but I see it as an advantage. The older students want to do Shakespeare, the younger ones just want to do a play. But we can do both with music, dance, asides, vignettes, clown shows, improvised shipwrecks, and all the magical people that Prospero can call forth.

I have a few specific ideas in mind. One is to begin by reading Leon Garfield's version of *The Tempest* to the young children. Garfield tells the stories of twelve plays in the book, skillfully weaving quotes from the plays into his narrative.

For the older students, we'll read Shakespeare while listening to a recording of the play. Recordings make theater much more accessible and provide a sense of rhythm and inflection that is very useful for learning to speak and act Shakespeare well.

I'd like to offer one word of caution, however. If you read Shakespeare, read the original, not one of the adaptations made for school use. I was tempted to use one in my preparation for *The Tempest*. At first I thought it was a condensation of Shakespeare's text for school performance and as such might save me the effort of doing my own adaptation. The script was in a book called *Shake Hands with Shakespeare*, published by Scholastic Press.

I wanted to begin my version of the play with Prospero and Miranda watching the tempest and the shipwreck, and so began reading Act I, Scene ii of the Scholastic version (out of laziness I think: it would have been just as easy to take the real Shakespeare off the shelf). The exchange between Miranda and Prospero bothered me. It was pedestrian, lacking Shakespeare's supple rhetoric and the elegance and appropriateness of his metaphors:

Enter Miranda and Prospero.
MIRANDA: If by your magic, my dearest father, you have caused this storm, please quiet the waters. O, I have suffered with those that I saw suffer. A brave vessel, who had no doubt some noble creatures in her, dashed all to pieces. Poor souls, they perished! Had I any power, I would have sunk the sea within the earth before it could have swallowed the good ship and the frightened souls within her.
PROSPERO: Collect yourself. Tell your piteous heart there's no harm done.
MIRANDA: Really, father?
PROSPERO: No harm. I have done nothing but for thy sake. My dear daughter, who knows not what thou art nor that I am more than just Prospero, master of a poor island.
MIRANDA: More to know did never enter my thoughts.
PROSPERO: 'Tis time I should tell thee more. Lend thy hand and pluck my magic garment from me. *(Takes off his cape.)*

I decided to look at Shakespeare after all and found the following:

Enter Prospero and Miranda.
MIRANDA: If by your art, my dearest father, you have
Put the wild waters in this roar, allay them.
The sky, it seems, would pour down stinking pitch,
But that the sea, mounting to the welkin's cheek,
Dashes the fire out. O, I have suffer'd
With those that I saw suffer! a brave vessel,
Who had, no doubt, some noble creature in her,
Dash'd all to pieces. O, the cry did knock
Against my very heart! Poor souls, they perish'd!
Had I been any god of power, I would
Have sunk the sea within the earth, or ere
I should the good ship so have swallow'd and
The fraughting souls within her.
PROSPERO: Be collected:
No more amazement: tell your piteous heart
There's no harm done.
MIRANDA: O, woe the day!

PROSPERO: No harm.
I have done nothing but in care of thee,
Of thee, my dear one, thee, my daughter, who
Art ignorant of what thou art, nought knowing
Of whence I am, nor that I am more better
Than Prospero, master of a full poor cell
And thy no greater father.
MIRANDA: More to know
Did never meddle with my thoughts.
PROSPERO: 'Tis time
I should inform thee farther. Lend thy hand,
And pluck my magic garment from me.—So:
[Lays down his mantle]

Shakespeare's "put the wild waters in this roar" had become "you have caused this storm" and

The sky, it seems, would pour down stinking pitch
But that the sea, mounting to the welkin's cheek
Dashes the fire out

disappears altogether. ("Welkin", according to the *Oxford English Dictionary*, means "the apparent arch or vault of heaven overhead . . . the region of the air in which the clouds float, the birds fly.")

The Tempest is made small in translation. I shared these two versions with some of my students recently and we discussed the differences; this turned out to be a wonderful lesson in understanding the poetic genius of Shakespeare. My advice for doing plays is to stick to the original and to do adaptations and modifications yourself and with your students. Too often "school" adaptations underestimate young people's ability to appreciate good literature.

If, after I read the story with students, they're interested in doing the play, I intend to draw a storyboard/map of the plot, and a graphic list of the cast of characters that indicates where each is when the play opens.

Here's my first draft of the dramatis personae:

Cast of Characters

ON THE ISLAND BEFORE THE SHIPWRECK

PROSPERO (a Wizard and the Duke of Milan)

MIRANDA (Prospero's daughter)
ARIEL (a delightful spirit who is bound to serve Prospero until re-
leased)
CALIBAN (a monster, original inhabitant of the island, and a slave of
Prospero's)

THE SHIPWRECKED CHARACTERS

ALONZO (King of Naples)
FERDINAND (Alonzo's son)
SEBASTIAN (Alonzo's brother)
ANTONIO (Prospero's brother, who stole his title of Duke of Milan)
GONZALO (an old man, counselor to the king)
TRINCULO & STEPHANO (servants and clowns)

ADDITIONAL CHARACTERS

SPIRITS
OFFICERS AND CREW OF THE SHIPWRECKED VESSEL

I'll also provide everyone with a condensed scenario describing
the flow of action.

The next step will be to begin improvisations based on the themes
of the play. I don't like to do the casting prematurely. It's best to get
everybody into the spirit of the play before discovering which particular role they would like to work on and perform. The first series
of improvisations will deal with storms and shipwrecks. One series
I've already experimented with involves the following scenario:

1. You are on a ship, sailing along peacefully when an unexpected tempest comes up and rocks the ship. Start slowly and hap-
pily at sea, and then as the sounds of the storm grow louder and
louder, move with the tossing ship and show your fear of being
drowned. The noises of the storm are made by shaking a sheet of
metal.

2. Your ship has sunk and you are thrown up on the shore of a
strange island. Improvise being thrown from the sea onto a sandy
beach. Remember: you are wet, frightened, and exhausted.

3. You pass out and then wake up very slowly, and feeling your
body to reassure yourself that you are still alive, slowly get up and
begin to look around.

95

Some other improvisations I plan to do will include monsters, flying, and invoking magical powers. I also plan to do improvisations using lines from the play:

O, wonder!
How many goodly creatures are there here!
How beauteous mankind is! O brave new world,
That has such people in 't!
(Act V, scene i)

Miranda has been stranded on an island for years with her father Prospero, and she has not seen other people. After the shipwreck, she encounters a number of men and expresses astonishment at the unexpected beauty—to her eyes—of even the ugliest of them. The improvisations will deal with the discovery of unexpected beauty and Shakespeare's lines will be worked into the scene. We might use fantasy worlds, or change the word "people" in the last line to "creatures" and play with the idea of the discovery of new and unexpected worlds.

These our actors
As I foretold you, were all spirits and
Are melted into air, into thin air.
And, like the baseless fabric of this vision,
The cloud-capp'd towers, the gorgeous palaces,
The solemn temples, the great globe itself,
Yea, all of which it inherit, shall dissolve
And, like this insubstantial pageant faded,
Leave not a rack behind. We are such stuff
As dreams are made on, and our little life
Is rounded with a sleep.
(Act IV, scene i)

This monologue is spoken by Prospero, who has put on a magical dance and feast and then realizes he has to end it quickly, because Caliban, Trinculo, and Stephano are plotting to kill him. This speech is both incantation and apology. I hope to have almost all of the students take a turn at reading it, at speaking Shakespeare. Most likely we will begin with Prospero's conjuring up a feast, mime the feast and entertainment (with mimed jugglers, dancers, musicians, chefs, waiters, etc.), and then have Ariel or some other character warn Prospero of danger. At this point, the speech will begin and the mime will turn to the theme of disappearance.

> . . . I'll break my staff,
> Bury it certain fathoms in the earth,
> And deeper than did ever plummet sound
> I'll drown my book.
> *(Act V, scene i)*

Thus does Prospero renounce his magical powers. These four lines call for the use of two props, a magic staff and a book of spells. I hope to find the right staff, one with some charisma, and a weighty ancient book, to use as props for the improvisation. Before denouncing magic, we'll experiment a lot with spells and enchantments, perhaps even returning to the beginning of the play and summoning up a tempest or two. Hopefully, everyone who cares to will get the feel of being Prospero.

These improvisations are meant to put the students in the mood to do *The Tempest.* They are meant to create an atmosphere of magic and intrigue, as well as to convey a sense of Shakespeare's language. Hopefully, they will also give students an opportunity to try many different parts without having to commit themselves to one. Of course there will be additional improvisations involving rulers, clowns, and all the other characters in the play. In the course of the improvisations and the readings, we'll talk about how to render the play. I'm confident that an interesting play will emerge, but at this moment I don't have the slightest idea of what the specifics will be.

There has been a recent and unexpected development, however. One of my high school students, Able, who is the bass guitarist in a local reggae band, said he might be interested in playing Prospero if the magic staff could be his bass guitar, which he could improvise on throughout the performance. Able is six feet four inches tall, and the idea of a tall, long-haired, bass-guitar-playing Prospero makes perfect sense to me. Now the challenge is to piece the play together while keeping this characterization in mind.

One of my other students has expressed interest in being Miranda. She's had a lot of experience acting and is creating a Miranda to go along with Able's Prospero. A few other members of the band said they might be interested in joining the cast, so there's a lot to work from.

I find myself always working on ideas for plays. The day after a performance, my mind starts working on the next play. A theater program does not end with a performance; new work builds on old successes and failures.

It's possible to adapt any play and it's also possible to do a play as it's scripted. Both ways of doing drama make sense. My preference is for adaptation because I find it an adventure, and because it frees me from the unenviable burden of deciding who's best for any given role.

The improvisational approach can be summarized as follows:

1. Read the play, not once but several times.

2. Summarize the story for your students. When possible, read the play with the group.

3. Identify the main themes in the play.

4. Develop improvisations based on these themes and on the characters.

5. Use excerpts from the play in some improvisations in order to familiarize the students with the language of the play.

6. Incorporate into the improvisation some of the props that figure in the action.

7. Watch what emerges from the students, and then pick a related scene from the play to work on. The scene can be chosen from any part of the play, but it should be one that can come together easily in the improvisations. Then work outward towards the whole play.

There are times when scenes push students' abilities to their limits. I've sometimes found that a scene or two from a play can be rendered beautifully by a group of youngsters, but that when I try to push towards the whole play the size of the venture is too great. As a consequence — since failure to perform can be devastating for some children — I've often done theater programs consisting of single scenes from different plays. One that worked beautifully with a group of junior high school students was called: *Scenes of Discovery.*

We did the scene from *Arsenic and Old Lace* where Mortimer discovers that his aunts are murderers; the scene from *The Bad Seed* where Rhoda's mother discovers that her daughter is a murderer; and the scene from *Cyrano de Bergerac* where Roxanne discovers that it is Cyrano and not Christian's words she has fallen in love with.

In doing drama with young people, what's important for me is that it be disciplined fun and lead to a performance that can be shared.

Chapter 5

Some Concluding Thoughts: On Cast Parties and Performances

When you do drama with young people, the first thing to plan is the cast party. The party has to be fun for the actors and technical crew as well as for parents and friends. Before beginning work on a play, I like to imagine the party, and think back from there to the steps necessary to get to that celebration. Thinking backwards in time allows me to anticipate what might go wrong and plan ways to avoid obvious mistakes.

First I imagine ways the cast party can fail. For example, someone might be sulking in the corner because he didn't get the part he wanted; or someone might be tense and angry because he wanted to participate but was afraid. Some parents might feel their children had been treated unfairly. Some students might feel that others had put them down for the minor roles they played, lines they forgot, or entrances they missed. The joy of being part of the theater can easily be lost in an atmosphere of jealousy and competition, and that's what I try to prevent. When doing theater with young people, you should pay as much attention to the pleasure of the participants as to the success of the performance. Successful cast parties become the criterion for the success of the whole theater program.

Moving backwards in time from the cast party to the performance, rehearsals, development of the script, and improvisations, try to imagine all of the mistakes that could prevent students from being part of an enjoyable experience that has contributed to their growth.

Some of the problems I've imagined emerging at the cast party are:

- A child who has refused to participate in the production stands in the corner sulking, or sneaks around the room spilling soda and insulting the actors. My fear of this makes me remember, even at the last possible moment, to push recalcitrant children into the production no matter how much they resist. Have them hold the script while you prompt, or have them knock on the stage three times to signal the beginning of the action, or have them put posters up in the community, take tickets, seat the audience, or be in charge of the costumes and props.

It doesn't make any difference how small the role is. What is essential is that every child have a sense of belonging, of being useful. Teachers have to learn how to create useful work for reluctant and scared children and to encourage them to take larger roles the next time around. Over the years, I've found that having a few unfilled jobs just before the performance provides the opportunity for even the most reluctant of students to help out and feel that the production could not happen without them.

- Jealousy is something to avoid at the cast party at all costs, even if it means four Alices, two Hamlets, twelve witches, or forty-eight dwarfs. Jealousy can spread throughout a cast party and throughout the class over the rest of the year, becoming a major impediment to learning. So I try to devise strategies to avoid the star syndrome and all of the disappointments that can emerge if someone doesn't get the part he wants. Again, one of the guiding principles of young people's theater is that it is not a route to TV or Broadway.

One way to get around the problem of jealousy is to provide every student who wants a part with one he or she feels is appropriate, and not to care how much revision or adaptation this may involve. Some people have told me my attitude is foolish, that I should pay more attention to teaching students how competitive and harsh the world is. My response is that I don't have to teach that—the kids already know it. I prefer to provide them with the love, success, and communal feelings that are all too lacking in that hard world everybody wants to prepare them for.

• Moving from the cast party back to the dress rehearsal, I try to figure out what specifically might go wrong. Lines might be forgotten; props can disappear at the last minute; the set could be only half finished by curtain time. Students have to be told this, and how to fake it when something goes wrong. I like to show the performers how to recover from disaster. Some recovery methods are:

• To keep on talking no matter what you're saying

• To use a prop, examine something on the set, and in general mutter about waiting for something important to happen

• To step out and talk to the audience out of character

• To begin a conversation with another actor on stage

• To tell the audience to be patient, and show your composure.

All of these depend upon having one person in each wing who is prompting and can be turned to for help, and another person whose specific job is to follow the script and hunt down missing actors.

It's better to anticipate disaster than encounter it unprepared. If someone misses an entrance, it's always possible to produce an instant monologue or dialogue while the director runs around looking for the absent or absconded actor. With five-, six-, and seven-year-olds this is a particular problem, as urinary and bowel control tends to decrease as performance time approaches. When you and the actors on stage anticipate this, the scared and incontinent ones can recover, perform, and have a good time at the cast party.

• The details of a dramatic performance are as important to young people as they are to members of the Royal Court Theatre or the New York Shakespeare Festival. Children who don't like their costumes or makeup, or who feel that their props are cheap and unconvincing, spend time apologizing for them and can be bores at cast parties. Therefore, it is of particular importance to ask actors to participate in the designing of makeup, costumes, and props.

• Performing is difficult for children who don't understand the play, and that means not just their roles, but the whole of the drama. To be able to feel good about what they have been a part of, they have to know what it is all about. Improvisation, discussion, and diagrams help give everyone a sense of the whole. All of the actors should know what is happening onstage when they are in the wings. This is especially true if you have adapted a play to the needs and personalities of your actors. One technique I've used during rehearsals is to have members of the cast who are not on stage sit in the audience and watch the action. I also encourage them to help me with blocking (deciding on the positions and movements of actors) and to make any suggestions for improving the performance. In addition, I act as a stand-in for the lead characters several times and have the actors watch from the audience so they can get a feel for what *they* might look like on stage. Then I suggest that the actors take turns directing scenes or parts of scenes. I encourage the fullest possible participation of the students in the whole process.

• Thinking of the cast party, you have to imagine the proud parents. Therefore you should think carefully about how to prepare an audience for student performance. A young person, who feels she or he has done very well and worked very hard, can be devastated by an offhand comment at a cast party. If your mother or father doesn't praise you, or if someone else's parents put you down, it can ruin the whole evening. For that reason, it is important to make it clear to parents that performance is part of the process of the development of imagination and, if necessary, make them realize that thinking that the school auditorium is just a step away from Broadway is not good for their children. Of course, the more you involve parents in small aspects of the performance and have them see and participate in improvisation, rehearsals, costumes, and sets, the more they will feel that they are part of what their children are doing. It is also good to involve them by having them prepare a potluck dinner for the cast party; after performing, children are hungry.

• A cast party can become a bore if only a few children get the credit for the performance. It takes a lot of effort to negate, at least in its most invidious forms, the gloating that children often indulge in when they think they're stars. Improvisations help because everyone gets to play all the roles in those informal exercises. If there are multiple performances of a play, I like to have different children play all the major roles in each performance. If the actors put down the tech crew, I'll turn off the lights and suggest the play be rehearsed in the dark. If they make fun of the prop master or the kids in charge of sound effects, they might find themselves fighting with invisible swords or waiting on stage, in the middle of a scene, for the sound of a phone call that never comes.

The goal is to create a sense of community through theater, one that just might spill over to the rest of the time the class spends together and even to life beyond the school.

• No matter how hard you try, there will be some kids who hate the cast party and won't be part of the play. It is important to learn that there are times when it will be impossible to get everyone involved. Expect trouble, and don't let it destroy the whole process. Keep on trying to get the most reluctant ones involved in the next performance or in the cast party itself. They can plan it, serve food, call parents, set tables. If none of this works, offer them a piece of cake and suggest that there is a good part for them in the next play. Or back off and see if poetry, mathematics, science, computers, music, or dance might be their modes of expression. And plan the next group activity so that you might have a better chance of getting them involved.

•

Recently I've been playing chess with five- to eight-year-olds. We have a chess club that meets once a week and I set up games so students can learn some of the sophistication of the game. A few weeks ago one of my students, Galen, who's six, beat me and, as proud as he was, tried to console me for losing. I laughed and told him that the goal of teaching is to have your students be decent people who are better and smarter than you are. It was a pleasure to see him acquire chess skills and use his mind in such sophisticated ways. That feeling was the same feeling I have when I see my students on stage, playing with ideas and taking control of their voices and bodies in ways I could never do. There is perhaps no greater pleasure one can get as a teacher than that of stepping back and grinning like a proud parent at the cast party of a play that has worked for everybody.

Appendix A
The Four Alices and Their Sister Susie

Opening: An Overture played by the band.
NARRATOR: Dear Gentle People. The Acorn Kids present The Four Alices and Their Sister Susie in Wonderland. Please join us.
(Lights come up on THE ALICES and SUSIE.)
NARRATOR: The Alices were beginning to get very tired sitting by their sister on the bank of the river, and of having nothing to do. Once or twice they peeped into the book their sister was reading, but it had no pictures or conversations in it, and they thought, "What is the use of a book without pictures or conversation?"
(Scene begins with ALICES listening to SUSIE read from the boring book.)
SUSIE: There once was a cat. It was a nice cat. It ran fast. It had nice fur. It was a fat cat...Alice. Alice. Pay attention. *(She looks around and sees THE ALICES.)*
SUSIE: Alice? Alice? Alice? *(THE FOURTH ALICE raises her hand and starts counting.)* 1...2...3...4 Alices. Who is the real Alice? Will the real Alice please stand up?
[Here the song "Will the Real Alice Please Stand Up?"]

Will the Real Alice Please Stand Up?

[*Note:* During this song the whole cast with the exception of THE ALICES sings everything but the words in quotation marks in the chorus parts. These are sung by THE ALICES.]

I'm so pretty
It's a pity

My necks's so long
From dusk to dawn

Chorus:
Will the real, real Alice
Please stand up.
"That's me." That's who?
"That's me." Uh huh.

Blond hair
Blue eyes
Can you tell me why
I grow so high

Chorus

My friend is mad
And he's so glad
The tea's not hot
And the mouse is in the pot

Chorus

What's the matter
With the Mad Hatter
Haven't you heard
He's crazy as a bird

Chorus

Why me
Can't you see
I'm so glad I'm Alice
In my palace

Chorus

NARRATOR: As this was going on, suddenly three white rabbits with pink eyes ran close by her. There was nothing so very remarkable in that. But when they noticed the rabbits' watches and umbrellas, they jumped to their feet. This was a most remarkable occurrence. The rabbits disappeared into rabbit holes and the Alices went after them.

(THE RABBITS enter, two from one side of the stage, one from the other. They bang into each other and play-fight and run off on the opposite side. THE ALICES jump down from the stage and two follow one rabbit and two follow the other two rabbits. SUSIE is left on stage by herself.)

(Here the song "I'm Alice's Sister")

[Editor's note: Song now lost.]

SUSIE: They can't have all the fun. Wait for me. I'm going too. *(She exits through the center of the curtain. Spot goes back to NARRATOR.)*

NARRATOR: The Alices chase the rabbits into a magical garden with fountains and trees and flowers. Green and yellow and red water flow from the fountain. The flowers and leaves are all the colors of the rainbow. The trees grow exotic fruits and candies. As the rabbits scurry away, the Alices find themselves before a large mushroom and a strange caterpillar.

(Curtain opens during the narration.)

(THE RABBITS run across the stage, one from each side. The mushroom and CATERPILLAR on it are set back a bit. THE RABBITS crash into each other once again, play-fight, and run off chattering.)

RABBITS: I'm late, I'm late for a very important date. I'm late, I'm late. . . .

(Following them from the wings are two ALICES from each side. THE ALICES run into each other, then see THE CATERPILLAR and scream and try to run away.)

CATERPILLAR:

"You are old, father William," the young man said,
And your hair is very very white;
And yet you stand on your head—
At your age do you think it is right?"

"In my youth," father William said to his son,
"I feared I might injure my brain;
But now that I'm sure I don't have one,
I do it again and again."

"You are old," said the youth, "one would hardly suppose
That your eye was as steady as ever;
Yet you balanced an eel on the end of your nose—
What made you so awfully clever?"

"I have answered one question and that is enough,"
Said his father. "Don't give yourself airs!
Do you think I can listen all day to such stuff?
Be off or I'll kick you down the stairs."

ALICES: *(bored)* Wonderful. . .could you tell us where the rabbits are going?
CATERPILLAR: To the Queen's party, stupids.
ALICES: *(now all together)* How do we get there?
CATERPILLAR: *(pointing in every direction)* That way, and that way and that way and that way.
ALICES: But. . .we'll get lost.
CATERPILLAR: Don't worry, all roads lead to the Queen.
(THE ALICES run off stage in different directions as the lights fade and the mushroom is transformed into a tree with THE CHESHIRE CAT staring down from one of its branches. As the lights go up again, THE ALICES run on from different parts of the wings and bump into each other as SISTER SUSIE comes strolling in.)
CHESHIRE CAT: *(with an enormous grin)* Hello Alice. . .Hello Alice. . .Hello Alice. . .Hello Alice. . .Hi Susie.
THE ALICES: Who are you?
SUSIE: Where did you come from?
CAT: *(Paying no attention to their questions)* I have a little story to tell and you can't have a story without some people to listen to it. It's so nice that you came to hear my story. It's about my cousin, Jabberwock. . .listen. . . .
" 'Twas brillig, and the slithy toves did gyre and gimble in the
    wabe.
All mimsy were the borogoves, and the mome raths outgrabe.
Beware the Jabberwock, my son! The jaws that bite. The claws
    that catch!
Beware the Jubjub bird and shun the frumious Bandersnatch!"

CHORUS: Come home, Alice......Alice, come on home
Don't stay too long in the looking glass
Alice, come home for supper, honey
CAT: "He took his vorpal sword in hand: long time the manxome foe he sought—so rested he by the Tumtum tree, and stood awhile in thought. And as in uffish thought he stood, the Jabberwock, with eyes of flame, came whiffling through the tulgey wood, and burbled as it came!
CHORUS: Come home, Alice......Alice, come on home
Don't stay too long in the looking glass
Alice, come home for supper, honey
CAT: One, two! One, two!
And through and through the vorpal blade went snicker-snack!
He left it dead, and with its head he went galumphing back.
And hast thou slain the Jabberwock? Come to my arms, my
     beamish boy!
O frabjous day! Callooh! Callay! He chortled in his joy.
CHORUS: Come home, Alice......Alice, come on home
Don't stay too long in the looking glass
Alice, come home for supper, honey
CAT: You like it?
ALICES and SISTER: *(less than excited)* Oh yes...of course... wonderful...inspired...brilliant.
SUSIE: Cat, can you tell me where I can go from here? This is all so confusing.
CAT: It doesn't matter which way you go...over there is a mad hatter...and over there is a mad mouse...you know in Wonderland we are all quite crazy...but never mind, just go on...they are waiting for you at the party....
(Curtain)

(Curtain opens. There is a long table. There are 11 chairs set around the table. THE MAD HATTER is sitting at the right end of the table. THE DORMOUSE is sleeping on the table. There are two empty seats next to THE MAD HATTER. The third seat along the table is occupied by THE DUCHESS. Under that seat is THE BABY, who is crying. Next to THE DUCHESS is DUNGEONS

AND DRAGONS—a form of Jabberwock. He is doing a lot of jab-bing.) The three white RABBITS come on. One from each side of the stage mumbling some things about being thirsty. They run around the table looking for a seat and finally the three of them sit down in the two chairs between THE HATTER and THE DUCH-ESS. They grab for tea cups. THE ALICES come in, two from each side. SUSIE walks in across the front of the stage.)

ALICES: A party...can we sit down...Please.

ALL SITTING AT THE TABLE: No room, no room....

MAD HATTER: Cut your hair...It's too messy...cut it now.

SUSIE: There's no need to make personal remarks...that's very rude.

MAD HATTER: *(With MOUSE and RABBITS nodding and com-menting—improvise these.)* Sit down. Sit down. Why is a raven like a writing desk?

SUSIE: *(as SUSIE and THE ALICES sit at the other end of the ta-ble)* Now we'll have some fun...a riddle.

ALICE: I love riddles...It's too hard....I think I heard that one before...It's impossible.

SUSIE: I believe I can guess that.

MAD HATTER: Do you mean you think you can find an answer to it?

SUSIE: Exactly so.

RABBITS *(together)*: Then you should say what you mean.

SUSIE: I do...at least I mean what I say...that's the same thing.

MAD HATTER: Not a bit. Why, you might as well say "I see what I eat" is the same thing as "I eat what I see."

DORMOUSE: Or that "I breathe when I sleep" is the same thing as "I sleep when I breathe."

DUCHESS and BABY: "Or I cried when I was born" is the same as "I'm born when I cry." *(BABY cries loudly.)*

RABBITS: Or that "I like what I get" is the same as "I get what I like."

ALICES: Why is a raven like a writing desk, anyway?

MAD HATTER: I don't have the slightest idea. What time is it?

RABBITS: *(taking out their watches, dipping them into tea cups)* Raining. Yes, raining time.

MAD HATTER: No. It's song time. I remember one. "Twinkle, twinkle."

ALL: *(with dance)*
Twinkle twinkle little bat
How I wonder where you're at
Up above the world so high
Like a tea tray in the sky

Chorus:
Twinkle twinkle little bat
How I wonder where you're at

Twinkle twinkle little rabbit
Why is being late your habit
You're always rushing here and there
But never getting anywhere

Chorus

Twinkle twinkle big fat queen
I wonder why you are so mean
You always scream "off with her head"
But if you do it, she'll be dead

Chorus

Twinkle twinkle Mister Hatter and hare
Teacups spilling everywhere
Everytime you drink you switch your cup
And then the dormouse fills it up

Chorus

Twinkle twinkle little Alice
We will never see you in a palace
Wonderland, it is so strange
When you're there you always change

Chorus

RABBITS: *(getting up and running around to THE ALICES as THE MAD HATTER dunks THE DORMOUSE into the teapot)* A message for you...and you...and you...and you...and *(to SU-SIE)* you too...the Queen commands your presence. Follow me. *(They run off in different directions and two ALICES follow each rabbit. SUSIE takes a last sip of tea, bids THE MAD HATTER and MOUSE goodbye and slowly walks off in the direction of the third RABBIT as the curtain closes.)*

(Curtain opens to the court of the QUEEN and KING OF HEARTS. Everyone is on stage with the exception of THE ALICES, SUSIE, and THE KING and QUEEN. Most actors are dressed as playing cards. Everyone is in costume. One RABBIT is standing on each side of the thrones of the KING and QUEEN, which are at center stage. The MOCK TURTLE is sitting off to one side and the GRIF- FIN off to the other. The RABBITS are executioners in this scene and they wave their boppers menacingly each time the QUEEN says "Off with their heads and feet." The court bows as the KING and QUEEN enter.)

QUEEN: *(Looks around and sees one card with the numbers painted backwards.)* Ignoramus! Off with his head! *(THE RABBITS wave their boppers. The MOCK TURTLE mocks the QUEEN. The KING puts his hand out for the QUEEN to take it and she forgets what she said.)*

KING: It's all right, dear. We must sit down. *(They go to their thrones and sit down.)*

QUEEN: On with the trial. Guilty. They're all guilty. Off with their heads and feet.

KING: But dear, no one's on trial.

QUEEN: Off with your head and feet.

KING: Come come, dear, calm down.

(THE ALICES and SUSIE enter from different places and ap- proach the throne.)

QUEEN: They're guilty. Off with their heads and feet.

ALICES: We didn't do anything. . . No, we didn't. . . No. . . Please.

MOCK TURTLE: They didn't do anything.

SUSIE: Everyone's mad around here.

MOCK TURTLE: Everyone's mad around here.

QUEEN: Of course, what did you expect in Wonderland?

MOCK TURTLE: What did you expect?

GRIFFIN: Off with their heads and feet.

QUEEN: No. Not yet. . . I need a story first.

KING: And a dance. . . always a dance before an execution.

GRIFFIN and MOCK TURTLE: A dance it is...All join in *(to ALICE and SUSIE)* You too...

"Will you walk a little faster?" said a whiting to a snail,

"There's a porpoise close behind us, and he's treading on my tail.

See how eagerly the lobsters and the turtles all advance!

They are waiting on the shingle—will you come and join the dance?

Will you, won't you, will you, won't you, will you join the dance?

Will you, won't you, will you, won't you, won't you join the dance?

"You can really have no notion how delightful it will be

When they take us up and throw us, with the lobsters, out to sea!"

But the snail replied, "Too far, too far!", and gave a look askance—

Said he thanked the whiting kindly, but he would not join the dance.

Would not, could not, would not, could not, would not join the dance.

Would not, could not, would not, could not, could not join the dance.

"What matters it how far we go?" his scaly friend replied.

"There is another shore, you know, upon the other side.

The further off from England, the nearer is to France—

Then turn not pale, beloved snail, but come and join the dance.

Will you, won't you, will you, won't you, will you join the dance?

Will you, won't you, will you, won't you, won't you join the dance?

(After the dance, the QUEEN and KING shout as THE RABBITS, MOCK TURTLE, MAD HATTER, CHESHIRE CAT, DORMOUSE, and GRIFFIN menacingly approach THE ALICES and SUSIE in slow motion. A little bit of background music here.)

QUEEN: Off with their heads and feet.

KING: Yes, off with their heads and feet.

GRIFFIN: Their heads.

MOCK TURTLE: Their feet.

MAD HATTER: Off with their tea.

DORMOUSE: Off with their meat.

CHESHIRE CAT: Off with them all.

RABBITS: Yes, yes, off off off.

ALICES: No...help...mommy...I want to go home.

SUSIE: *(very loud, causing everyone to go silent)* Wait...wait...
You're nothing but a deck of cards.

ALICES: *(together)* A deck of cards.

(THE WHOLE COURT screams and starts throwing cards up in the air and running around, shouting.)

ALL: We're nothing but a deck of cards. We're nothing but a deck of cards. We're nothing but a deck of cards....

(The curtain closes.)

NARRATOR: At this the whole pack of cards rose up in the air and came flying down on THE ALICES and SUSIE. They screamed, half from fright and half from anger, and as they tried to escape the cards, they found themselves back on the bank of the river.

(THE ALICES and SUSIE come rushing out from the center of the curtain and sit down, panting.)

ALICES: What a curious dream. We have to go home.

(THE ALICES get up and walk off.)

SUSIE: I'm not so sure. I'm going back.

NARRATOR: And so Susie stepped back into Wonderland and found herself in a looking glass world...but that's another story for another day....

(Band plays refrain of songs as the curtain opens and EVERYONE takes a bow.)

Appendix B
Antigone

Adapted by Herbert Kohl and Sande Zeig

(Open a bare stage. Enter from the left CALLIOPE, the Greek muse of storytelling.)

CALLIOPE: Euterpe, Euterpe, are you and Erato ready? And where is Terpsichore?

(From behind stage the sounds of music.)

EUTERPE and ERATO: Just a few more minutes.

CALLIOPE: *(to audience)* You'll have to forgive my sisters, ladies and gentlemen. It is not always easy to bring the Muses together.

(Enter from stage right CLIO, URANIA, and POLYHYMNIA carrying a throne. They place the throne on the platform.)

CLIO: Here is where it happened, this is the historical place, Thebes, 32 miles from Athens, over 3,000 years ago.

URANIA: But it happened in the stars, too—the story of Oedipus and his unhappy family was made in heaven as well as on earth.

CLIO: The play of the gods (POLYHYMNIA *mimes the action as the narrative continues)* affected the people in unexpected and not always happy ways.

CALLIOPE: We Greeks are a story-telling people and many of our stories. . . .well, they combine things in ways that may seem new and strange to you.

(THALIA *and* MELPOMENE *enter from behind the stage with their masks.)*

CALLIOPE: You see my sisters Thalia and Melpomene, they have different ways of looking at the world and yet they are part of the story.

115

THALIA: Tonight my laughter is the laughter of the gods, our relatives. The family is large and not always happy but we don't have to worry about our disputes.

MELPOMENE: Of course you immortals don't, that's why you can be foolish and playful and never tragic. Tragedy is only possible where life ends in death. I take the part of the mortals, those poor creatures whose life is built so delicately and can disappear in a second. You may be partial to the gods, I weep for Oedipus and his children.

CALLIOPE: But this may be getting too far ahead of the story. . . . *(looks about in an agitated way)* Euterpe, are you and your sisters ready. . .we can't keep these people waiting any more.

(Music is heard off stage and then the MUSES OF SONGWRITING *come on stage. ALL THE SISTERS* sit and the three sing and dance a choral ode to be composed by the actors.)

CALLIOPE: And so now ladies and gentlemen we have brought the arts together.

ERATO: Have fused music, dance, and composition.

URANIA: Have added science and the mystical.

THALIA: Will dare to be comic.

MELPOMENE: And tragic.

CLIO: Will show you some of history.

CALLIOPE: And tell a good and complex tale. . .bring on the gods.

(GODS enter. CLOWN show.)

(ZEUS is on roof of shed with the bottles of GOOD QUALITIES *and* EVIL FEATURES *on either side of a throne.)*

ZEUS: The ingredients for Antigone are supposed to be a little bit of this and a lot of that, since no one is perfect.

HERA: *(enters, holding a book)* Zeus, you've made a mistake again, *(she refers to the book)* there is supposed to be a lot of good and only a little evil in Antigone. Look for yourself.

ZEUS: *(looks at the book)* Baa. I'm Zeus and no one can tell me that I am wrong. Go away, Hera.

HERA: You'll see if you can get away with being unjust. *(She exits.)*

(Then ZEUS exits. POSEIDON and ATHENA enter. They are arguing.)

POSEIDON: I deserved to be patron of Attica, not you Athena.

ATHENA: All of that was decided a long time ago, Poseidon. Stop crying over trivialities. Zeus made a fair decision.

(HERMES *and* ARGOS *enter.)*

HERMES: Zeus told me to kill you Argos (ARGOS *laughs)* but maybe we should just become friends. (ARGOS *picks* HERMES *up in his arms.)*

(EROS *and* ARES *enter together.)*

EROS: Here is the apple of discord, Ares.

ARES: Oh, no, please Eros, take that away from me. I don't really want to fight right now.

(DIONYSUS, HERA, *and* ECHO *enter.)*

HERA: If you don't mind, Dionysus, the feast will have to wait until after the meeting.

ECHO: The feast will have to wait until after the meeting.

DIONYSUS: A little wine will only help pass the time quickly. Is Zeus going to be here, too?

ECHO: Is Zeus going to be here, too?

HERA: No.

ECHO: No.

DIONYSUS: Oh.

HERA: Now gods and goddesses of Olympus, Zeus is once again being unjust. We must not allow this.

ECHO: Unjust and we must not allow this.

ATHENA: What is the accusation?

HERA: He is changing history.

ALL: *(upset and surprised)* Oh, my. . . . Who is changing the story . . .? What is the story?

ARES: Did someone say gory?

POSEIDON: Well, then what should we do?

HERA: We should put him in chains until he becomes just.

HERMES: Now that's a good idea. (DIONYSUS *has been giving him some drinks.)*

ATHENA: Why don't we ask him to listen to reason first?

HERA: Because he refuses to.

ECHO: Because he refuses to.

EROS: Why don't you be quiet, Echo?

ECHO: Why don't you be quiet, Echo?

ARES: I am all for revolt as long as it is non-violent.

(ZEUS *enters.)*

HERA: Throw him in chains.

ATHENA: Grab his legs.

ARES: Ow, that hurt.

DIONYSUS: Pass the wine please?

HERMES: Certainly.

POSEIDON: We've got him. (ZEUS *is put in chains.)*

ZEUS: What is the meaning of this?

ECHO: What is the meaning of this?

DIONYSUS: Now that the tyrant is in chains, let's have a feast with music and dancing.

ATHENA: And let's hope that Antigone fends as well against her oppressors.

HERA: She will.

ECHO: She will this time.

(ALL OF THE GODS *appear on the roof of the shed [Mount Olympus]. They all dance, and above them on Olympus* ALL THE GODS *and* GODDESSES *dance on the roof.* MUSES *throughout will bring the props on and off stage, occasionally improvising comments. After the clown show is over the* CHORUS *enters.)*

CHORUS: There they are, the fools, the clowns, enjoying their immortal lives, while here on the road to Thebes, poor, rash Oedipus learns of his fate from a blind seer.

(TIRESIAS, *obviously blind, comes on stage left while* OEDIPUS *enters from the right and bumps into* TIRESIAS.)

OEDIPUS: Out of the way, fool.

TIRESIAS: *(composed and quietly)* In this short life only those who rush are fools.

OEDIPUS: What are you talking about?

TIRESIAS: I see you rushing to your destruction. Pause a while with me.

OEDIPUS: Out of the way. *(He rushes off stage left,* TIRESIAS *goes off to the right.)*

CHORUS: And so Oedipus came to Thebes, and met the Sphinx, the feared monster that kept the city dark and hungry.

SPHINX: *(looking at Oedipus)* Another mortal. . . .What are you doing here? Do you expect you will do any better than the rest?

OEDIPUS: *(reaching for his sword)* I challenge you.

SPHINX: The challenge is for your mind. . . .What is it that walks on four legs in the morning, two legs at noon, and three legs in the evening?

OEDIPUS: *(after thinking for a bit)* It is a person, a babe crawling at the dawn of life, a man or woman walking through noon, and leaning on a cane in the evening of life.

SPHINX: How did you. . .how could you. . . .(SPHINX *dies.)*

CHORUS: And so Oedipus, at the moment of his triumph, entered Thebes.

CHORUS 2: Only to find that his victory was his defeat.

CHORUS: He married and had four children, two daughters, Antigone and Ismene. . .

CHORUS 2: And two sons, Polynices and Eotocles.

MELPOMENE: *(emerging from the back of the stage with her tragic mask)* Poor Oedipus discovered he had killed his father on the road to Thebes, and that the Queen was his mother. Unable to bear the pain, Oedipus blinded himself and set out with his daughters to atone for his sins.

(OEDIPUS *and* FOUR CHILDREN *on stage.* OEDIPUS *is now blind.)*

OEDIPUS: This is my moment to leave. Daughters, Ismene, Antigone, come with this poor, old blind man and help me seek peace. . .and you my sons, rule well. Each of you rule for a year, take turns at being just and good for the people of Thebes, for they have suffered enough. You, Eotocles, rule first and rule well. And you, Polynices, come with me a bit and travel and learn, so that when you return to Thebes you may rule well.

(OEDIPUS, ANTIGONE, ISMENE, POLYNICES *leave and* EOTOCLES *slowly rises and sits on the throne, as* TIRESIAS *enters downstage.)*

TIRESIAS: Thus Oedipus ended his life in exile, seeing no better than the outside world and understanding too much of the inner. . . .He left his sons to rule but they were no more able to share power than most mortals.

(Enter CREON, JOCASTA, *and* HAEMON.)

CREON: Nephew, let me have a word with you.

JOCASTA: Your year of ruling is near an end.

CREON: And yet you make a most wonderful king.

HAEMON: It is true, cousin.

EOTOCLES: *(thoughtfully)* And what do you suggest?

CREON: Continue to rule.

JOCASTA: Destroy your worthless brother.

HAEMON: I hear he has brought seven armies against us, that is no gesture of friendship.

CREON: Let us meet him on the plain.

JOCASTA: And Thebes shall be ours.

URANIA: And thus they did decree.

CLIO: And history did prove.

URANIA: That neither of the brothers would rule long.

CLIO: They met and fought and died, leaving Thebes to Creon and Jocasta, and their son Haemon.

THALIA: And the gods laughed to see such a waste of life.

(There is a battle scene ending in the death of the two brothers— needs lots of music and action—perhaps the MUSES can make some and the GODS comment on the foolishness of mortals fighting. The scene ends with all the corpses offstage except that of POLYNICES.) (CALLIOPE enters carrying a raven which she places on a stump.)

CALLIOPE: And thus after the battle all the soldiers were given honorable burial.

POLYHYMNIA: All, that is, except Polynices, that brother who never did get to rule.

CALLIOPE: King Creon threw his body to the vultures and ravens.

POLYHYMNIA: Insulted him and disgraced his family.

CALLIOPE: Which with the death of Oedipus left only the sisters, Antigone and Ismene, who returned sadly to Thebes after their father's death.

POLYHYMNIA: Only to find more death. Two brothers gone.

CALLIOPE: And one disgraced.

(Enter from ramp on left ANTIGONE and ISMENE.)

ANTIGONE: Can this be poor Polynices, our brother?

ISMENE: I heard in the city that King Creon has put his body out for the vultures. He said it was punishment for defying his royal power.

120

ANTIGONE: We must bury our brother.

ISMENE: I'm not so sure. Creon and Jocasta have enormous tempers. Besides, one has to obey the king.

ANTIGONE: There are more important things than kings. I have to bury Polynices. I owe it to our family and to the higher law that says every person is special and has to be respected. I'm not afraid of Creon, or Jocasta, or that son of theirs.

(Enter CREON, JOCASTA, and HAEMON.)

JOCASTA: Did I hear our names, Antigone?

CREON: Welcome back to Thebes.

ANTIGONE: I intend to bury my brother with respect.

CREON: You'll do no such thing.

JOCASTA: The birds will be just as happy with your flesh as with that of your brothers.

ANTIGONE: I intend to bury Polynices. Will you stand with me, sister?

ISMENE: I...I...don't know.

ANTIGONE: I intend to bury my brother. Will you stand with me, Haemon?

HAEMON: Well...Father, Mother...what difference can it make that he be buried honorably?

CREON: The law is the law.

JOCASTA: Royal law stands absolute and alone.

ANTIGONE: I will bury my brother. The moral law is higher than the law of kings....Will you stand with me, Haemon...Ismene?

ISMENE: We stand together.

HAEMON: Father, Mother, I honor you, but I do not honor kings. I must stand with Antigone.

(THE THREE draw swords, as do CREON and JOCASTA, and they duel. THE THREE win, walk slowly up to the throne, and carry it off stage.) (The MUSES and CHORUSES return.)

CHORUS: The time of kings is short.

CALLIOPE: The time of people ruling together may be near.

MUSES: The time for song and dance is here.

(A melody. ALL leave stage slowly.)

THE END

Selected Resources

On the Theory and Practice of Doing Plays

Boleslavsky, Richard. *An Actor Prepares* (New York: Theatre Arts Books, 153 Waverly Place, New York, NY 10014). This well-written book provides specific exercises and is particularly good on ways of expressing emotion on stage. It would be useful to ask for the Theatre Arts Books catalog, a list of wonderful resources for teachers.

Cole, Toby and Chinoy, Helen Krich. *Actors on Acting* (New York: Crown, 1970). This is an anthology of writing about acting, ranging from Aristotle to Julian Beck and Judith Malina to the Bread and Puppet Theater. It is full of insights about ways in which people have gone about acting and thinking about acting.

Hoggett, Chris. *Stage Crafts* (New York: St. Martin's Press, New York: 1975). This book is a must. It is full of diagrams and information about the construction of sets, the design of props and costumes, the application of makeup, and the use of lighting. It is an amateur theater person's encyclopedia.

Lawson, John Howard. *Theory and Technique of Playwrighting* (New York: G. P. Putnam, 1936). This is one of the finest books on playwriting, but unfortunately it is difficult to get. It is worth a trip to the library.

Spolin, Viola. *Improvisation for the Theater* (Evanston: Northwestern University Press, 1987). Along with *Stage Crafts*, this is a must for teachers of children's theater. It is arguably the best book ever written on improvisation.

Sources for Scenes

The four inexpensive volumes below contain about 200 scenes from plays written over the last 2,000 years throughout the world. They provide wonderful preliminary script reading exercises and are arranged by the number and gender of the actors in each scene, and could even be used as basic texts for introductory classes on theater.

Schulman, Michael and Mekler, Eva. *The Actor's Scenebook*, Vols. I and II (New York: Bantam Books, 1984 and 1987).

Steffensen, James L. *Great Scenes from World Theater*, Vols. I and II (New York: Avon Books, 1968 and 1972).

Shakespeare

For the development of a theater program, an edition of the complete works of Shakespeare is a necessity. There are many editions, some in one big volume, others in individual volumes. I use either the *Arden Shakespeare* (University Paperbacks) or the *Pelican Shakespeare* (Penguin Books), though the *Yale Shakespeare* and other editions are also excellent. Look around for the format, annotation, and print size that you feel most comfortable with.

Garfield, Leon. *Shakespeare's Stories* (New York: Schocken Books, 1985). This book contains well-written retellings of the plot and substance of twelve of Shakespeare's plays. It has been published as a children's book and is entertaining and full of memorable quotations from Shakespeare. I find it a good text to work from when introducing youngsters to Shakespeare, as well as a resource for the adaptation of Shakespeare's plays for performance by my students.

Sher, Anthony. *Year of the King* (New York: Limelight Editions, 1987). This is a personal account by a great English actor of what he went through when preparing to play Richard III. It is very lively and moving, and reveals the struggles of a professional actor in a dramatic and quite literate way. I think it makes great reading for young actors.

Illustrations

In swordplay...

...turnabout is fair play.

Puck in *A Midsummer Night's Dream*

Developing *A Midsummer Night's Dream*

Cover of *The Four Alices* playbill

YOU ARE CORDIALLY
INVITED TO A
PERFORMANCE OF
A MIDSUMMER
   NIGHT'S DREAM.

A   POT   LUCK
DINNER   AND
JAM   SESSION
WILL   FOLLOW :

PLEASE   BE ON TIME 4·30PM
FRIDAY   JUNE 29, 1979

Invitation to *A Midsummer Night's Dream*

127

Haemon in *Antigone*

The gods on high mock human folly in *Antigone*

The Muses in *Antigone*

The narrator, one of the Alices, and her sister Susie

"You're nothing but a deck of cards!" (from *The Four Alices* dress rehearsal)

The two Cheshire Cats in *The Four Alices*

Plastic pipe makes versatile stage sets in adaptation of Thurber's *Little Red Riding Hood*

The Royal Court in *The Four Alices*

Mime Sande Zeig *(left)* demonstrates pantomime with Kohl for Moliere's *Tartuffe*

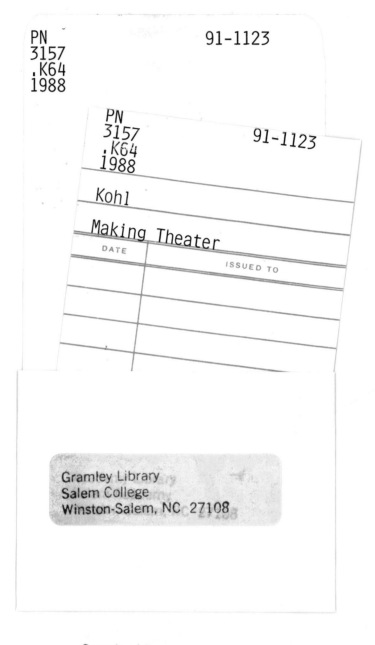